Oracle8 Design Tips

Oracle8 Design Tips

Dave Ensor and Ian Stevenson

Cambridge · Köln · Paris · Sebastopol · Tokyo

Oracle8 Design Tips
by Dave Ensor and Ian Stevenson

Copyright © 1997 O'Reilly & Associates, Inc. All rights reserved.
Printed in the United States of America.

Editor: Deborah Russell

Production Editor: Jane Ellin

Printing History:

September 1997: First Edition.

This book is printed on acid-free paper with 85% recycled content, 15% post-consumer waste. O'Reilly & Associates is committed to using paper with the highest recycled content available consistent with high quality.

ISBN: 1-56592-361-8   [10/97]

Table of Contents

Preface

Why did we write this little book—and why so soon after publishing our first book, *Oracle Design?* Of course, the answer is timing. Within months after our first book (based primarily on Oracle7) came out, Oracle Corporation finally set a date for the release of Oracle8. Why didn't we just wait for Oracle8? We knew that Oracle8 was coming, but the release had been years in the making and nobody knew exactly when it would finally emerge. It didn't really make sense to wait. We had a lot to say about Oracle7 and we believed that almost all of our advice would still be applicable to Oracle8. Now that we've seen the new release, we can verify that the recommendations in *Oracle Design* are, in most cases, still appropriate.

However, we didn't want to leave it at that. The announcement of Oracle8 represents Oracle's most significant advance in many years. Oracle8 offers a large number of new features, and it overcomes many design limitations present in Oracle7, giving designers more options than they have had in the past. We decided to write a small update to our basic book—a set of design tips focused only on the Oracle8 features that designers (and others concerned about how good design results in good performance) would need to be concerned about. These features give us better choices of design options than were available in Oracle7 (although some of them should carry health warnings!). In the best cases, the new features mean less work for both designers and developers. Features such as partitioned tables now provide implicit support for an approach that previously would have required the designer to come up with a solution.

There has been a good deal of hype about Oracle8, and the wait for the new version has been a long one. Many people had anticipated a radical move from a relational to an object-oriented DBMS. But as it turns out, the server technology is still very much based on a relational database. Those of us who have worked with Oracle for many years aren't too surprised. Oracle moves into new technologies in an evolutionary, rather than a revolutionary, fashion. And Oracle has always been concerned about how new releases would affect its large base of existing customers. Those customers can't simply dump their existing Oracle applications for a new solution—however wonderful the solution may be. But everyone will find something in Oracle8 that they can use. There are some features of Oracle8 that existing Oracle7 applications can exploit without a complete rewrite, and some that can be exploited simply by installing the new version. There are also a number of Oracle8 features that will produce significant savings for new projects for the cost of a small change or refinement in the design.

We wrote this book to supplement, rather than replace, our original book. Most of the principles and guidelines we described in that first book still apply. In fact, much of the advice in that book is essentially database-independent. We've even heard from a few Sybase designers who have used the advice to good effect! In this small update, we don't cover general design issues at all; we concentrate simply on the effects on design of the new features within Oracle8.

A word of caution: Because of the timing of the release and our desire to get the book out as early as possible in its life cycle, the book was developed mainly using beta copies of the software. Although the code was late in the beta cycle, we can't guarantee that all the features we describe here actually made it into the production version as is. In addition, some of the terminology was subject to very late revision and was not reflected in the beta manuals and software we were using. Version numbers were rationalized late in the day, so SQL*Net Version 3 became Net8, and PL/SQL Version 3 became PL/SQL8. We hope that we have caught most of the changes, and we apologize for any we may have missed. Oracle uses its beta test programs to thoroughly quality-assure the software in terms of both robustness and functionality. Features that fail to meet the acceptance criteria are either fixed or are deferred to a later release. As with Oracle7.1, we expect Oracle8.1 to be rich with many new features that didn't quite make it into Oracle8.0.

NOTE	Although we focus on the new Oracle8 features in this book, we hope that you won't get so embroiled in the new features that you lose site of the bigger picture. Remember your overall goal—you are trying to design an application or a product using this technology.

One of the nicest features of learning Oracle8 has been the quality and coverage of the documentation set. Neither of us possess a single hardcopy Oracle8 manual; instead, we've been using the HTML version of the manuals, which we loaded onto our Windows NT machines along with the software. Gone, thank goodness, is Oracle Book (perhaps the world's least attractive documentation reader). Our praise of the documentation does beg the question: If the manuals are so good and cover so much, why not rely on your online copies of the manuals? Why should you read (let alone buy) this book? Here are three good reasons:

1. There is simply too much to read. Even just starting with the excellent *Oracle8 Server Concepts* manual is intimidating. And there are 14 more large manuals in the server set! As a designer you don't need to know at the outset how to make every last feature work. Our book is short and to the point. It introduces you to the new features that we believe (based on our experience) should result in real changes to your design approach.

2. Some of the documentation is misleading. There are descriptions in the manuals which may cause you to waste a great deal of time and money. We'd like to save you the pain that we've experienced puzzling out some of the features.

3. We are really nice people with families, pets, and all that, and O'Reilly won't pay us if the book does not sell.

OK, only two good reasons.

Structure of This Book

Oracle8 Design Tips is organized as follows:

- Chapter 1, *What's New in Oracle8?*, provides a brief overview of the new features of Oracle8 and discusses why Oracle has moved in the direction that it has with the new release.

- Chapter 2, *Methodologies for Oracle8*, compares the use of traditional methodologies and analysis and design tools with that of object-oriented development. It also looks briefly at the role of the Network

Computer Architecture (NCA) in moving towards more component-based development projects.

- Chapter 3, *Miscellaneous Oracle8 Enhancements*, describes a number of important Oracle8 features that have an impact on design (but that don't fit into the categories covered in Chapter 4 or Chapter 5).

- Chapter 4, *Oracle8's "Big" Features*, looks at the significant advances made in supporting very large databases (VLDBs) and a large number of concurrent users.

- Chapter 5, *Objects*, surveys the main Oracle8 object features, considers the level of object orientation that can be realistically achieved with the current release, and comments on the extent to which Oracle8 supports the object paradigm.

- Chapter 6, *Tool Support for Oracle8*, looks at what tools are available for Oracle8 and does some crystal ball gazing into what may be coming.

Comments and Questions

All of the information about Oracle8 is still very new. We'll be seeing bug fixes and new versions soon. Although we hope that our basic design advice will stand the test of time, you may find that some of the details must change for future releases of Oracle8. We also hope that some of the deficiencies we've pointed out may be fixed in future releases.

Please address comments and questions concerning this book to the publisher:

> O'Reilly & Associates
> 101 Morris Street
> Sebastopol, CA 95472
> 1-800-998-9938 (in the U.S. or Canada)
> 1-707-829-0515 (international or local)
> 1-707-829-0104 (FAX)

You can also send us messages electronically. See the insert at the back of the book for information about all of O'Reilly's online services.

Acknowledgments

Both the authors and the editor especially want to record their gratitude to David Saxby of Oracle Corporation for performing a comprehensive and detailed review of the book in a very short amount of time.

Dave would like to extend special thanks to Sanjeev Kumar, Keith Rushto, and Peter Vasterd of Oracle for their enthusiasm and willingness to answer questions during his Oracle8 training course.

Thanks to all the people at O'Reilly & Associates who turned our manuscript into a book in record time: to Debby Russell our editor; Jane Ellin our production editor; Mike Sierra who converted our Word files into Frame; Kimo Carter who formatted and entered edits into the files; Robert Romano who created the figures; Edie Freedman and Nancy Priest who designed the cover and interior format; and PageMasters & Company who did final production and packaging of the book.

Dave would like to thank his wife Mefus for her "understated response" when she learned that he and Ian were writing a second book and for her support through a very busy spring and summer. Ian would once again like to thank his wife Brenda and his children Todd and Tara for their unfaltering support during the hard slog. He promises them a vacation, eventually...

1

What's New in Oracle8?

Oracle8 is finally here. What's in the new version and does it live up to expectations?

In this chapter we look at what Oracle8 is—and what it is not. We examine the message that the Oracle marketers are putting out and ponder what it means to us. We also outline what we consider to be the most significant features of Oracle8 (significant both from the perspective of wearing our designers' hats and from our expectation of what features will most heavily be used). We also believe that some features of Oracle8 won't play a major role in Oracle8 projects—only time will tell if we are right.

Oracle's Marketing Message

This past summer, one of us had the pleasure of attending the spectacular launch of Oracle8. Larry Ellison, Oracle's CEO, was at his best, giving live demonstrations and sniping at Microsoft. That part wasn't surprising. What was surprising was the fact that the event focused much more than anticipated on Oracle's vision of a new age of computing—network computing. We had expected the technical features and the much-touted object technology of Oracle8 to be on display. Instead, the network computer (NC), rather than the database, was the star.

What are we to make of Oracle's new initiative? Reading between the lines, we're seeing the Oracle database becoming something of a commodity—something that we'll simply take for granted. The analogy is simple: when you turn a tap on, you expect the water to flow; you don't want to worry about how it got there. Similarly, when you turn your computer on, you expect the data and applications to be there as a matter of course. You don't care where the data and applications physically reside, and you don't care how they make their way to you.

Oracle is clearly positioning Oracle8 as more than just a database; it is now being regarded as a file server as well. The overwhelming message of the company: the cost of computing is coming down; it's more reliable and more secure to have an Oracle8 database storing and delivering your data than it would be to use conventional methods (a mixture of local client hard drives and shared files on a server file system). This world view puts the onus on Oracle designers—as never before—to ensure that the expectations and needs of the users are satisfied.

Originally, Oracle8 was being described as a fully featured object database. There certainly is a move towards object support, but the emphasis has most definitely changed. Oracle has clearly listened to its existing customers and has paid attention to what they want.[*] In subsequent chapters, we'll describe the many new features released with Oracle8. However, when you come right down to it, Oracle8 is primarily a robust, scalable, database management system that is capable of holding huge volumes of data and delivering it cost-effectively, reliably, and securely to large user communities. Anything more is just icing on the cake!

The architecture that is Oracle's vision of the future of computing is shown in Figure 1-1.

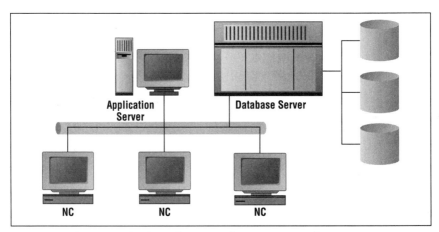

Figure 1-1: The essentials of Oracle's Network Computing Architecture

---

[*] It also appears that the company has observed the problems that Informix has been experiencing.

At first glance, you might not see anything revolutionary. But there is one main difference from anything we've seen before: the lack of any local disk for the network computer. NCs are low-cost items; they may not even be conventional "computers," but instead, microprocessors that control such things as heating systems. The main point of them is this: *all* the data resides on the database server—sales ledgers, spreadsheets, images, pictures, video clips, or whatever. The application server contains all the executable code that can be downloaded and run on the NCs. Of course, the NCs might be the PCs you already have on your desks. However, you won't be using your hard disks for data and program storage any longer. Holding all applications software on the application server makes software maintenance much simpler—for example, an upgrade will immediately apply to all users. It will also be much easier to control who runs what software and to protect against infection from viruses

Oracle8 Features

Back to earth. Oracle8 has arrived with a good many features that will help Oracle sell its new vision and will also remedy some of the restrictions users and developers have had in the past. This section provides a brief summary of the new technical features within Oracle8 in the context of the marketing message we've described. These features (and their claimed benefits) include:

- *Scalability.* Oracle8 supports much more data and many more users than Oracle7, and it runs a good deal faster.

- *Reliability.* Oracle8 runs and recovers more reliably than Oracle7.

- *Security.* Oracle8 has better security features than Oracle7.

- *Data.* In Oracle8, data can be managed more easily. You can maintain more copies of it, represent it in additional ways, and access it more quickly.

- *Object orientation.* Oracle8 doesn't get us all the way to a truly object-oriented system, but it's a good first step. If offers object types and object views with various ways to manipulate object data.

In the following chapters, we'll expand on many of these features. In particular, we'll focus on new or improved areas where you'll need to make design decisions and choose what's best for your application. Design is all about choosing the best alternative from what's available. With the new features provided by Oracle8, Oracle Corporation is giving us a good many additional alternatives from which to choose.

Scalability

Many users of Oracle7 have hit size limitations and have had to split their data and users between servers. Oracle Corporation claims that Oracle8 provides a tenfold size improvement in Oracle8 (compared with Oracle7). Let's look at each of the specific claims and see how they stack up.

- Oracle8 can support ten times the amount of data.

  This claim appears to be completely justified. There are sufficient changes to both the internal structures and the ways in which large objects are handled to permit databases to stretch into tens of terabytes of data—a frightening amount! Individual tables can now have up to 1000 columns, whereas Oracle7 limited you to 254.

  In addition, the database can now support very large objects, known as *LOB*s. A single occurrence of a LOB can hold up to four gigabytes of data. The data can even be external to the database.

- Oracle8 can support ten times as many users.

  Oracle claims to have achieved support for a larger user community, mainly by reducing the per-user memory overhead on the server by between 30 and 60%. We frankly doubt that savings of this order can be achieved across the board. Even if they are achieved, we'll bet that such savings are going to be barely sufficient to allow current servers to handle double the number of users, let alone ten times the number of users.

  Other new support in this area includes server-based queuing technology (which allows updates to be stored for later delivery) and a messaging facility within the server (which can be used to take on the tasks that were traditionally achieved by middleware). Note that moving the load traditionally imposed by middleware onto the same hardware as the database server is not, at first glance, a recipe for being able to support more users

- Oracle8 is up to ten times faster.

  Based on past experience, we would advise you not to take this highly attractive claim at face value. There are certainly some cases where it will be true. For example, performing queries against partitioned data warehouse tables which have equi-partitioned bitmap indexes should run much faster than the same queries under Oracle7. Why? Because the CPU burden of executing the query can be segregated and divided among available CPUs and I/O processors. We don't doubt that some database operations will be "up to" ten times faster. But we expect that most existing applications will find that most of their SQL statements will run at almost the same speed under Oracle8 as they did under Oracle7. Life is like that.

Does this sound as if we're negative about Oracle8? Not at all. We see a great many features in Oracle8 which we are confident that all of us will be able to use to implement larger, faster, more reliable, and more available applications. We are just a little skeptical about claims of tenfold improvements across the board.

Reliability

If the database is going to replace local disk storage, then reliability is a must. In today's client server computing world, most of us can find some useful work to do on our PCs even if the network or server is down. What would happen in the new world? An advance in technology can't mean a retrograde step in terms of reliability remember our tap and water analogy.

Oracle8's reliability is built around such technologies as these:

- The Oracle Parallel Server product
- Disk mirroring
- Fast and simple recovery mechanisms

Enhancements in Parallel Server support allow Oracle to recover from the failure of one of the servers without requiring any manual intervention and with a minimal disruption to service.

In the rare event of a major failure—one in which data is lost—Oracle8's recovery is much faster than Oracle7's. Oracle8's recovery from archived redo logs has been enhanced to use multiple processors. In addition, a new GUI wizard-driven interface greatly reduces the chance of human error during the recovery process. The wizard is part of the new *Recovery Manager* (described in Chapter 3, *Miscellaneous Oracle8 Enhancements*) which makes the whole task of managing backup and recovery a lot simpler than it was in the past. Because it automates backup and recovery, the Recovery Manager is a true godsend for database administrators.

Oracle8 also provides a new utility, *DB_VERIFY,* which ensures the logical integrity of the data in an Oracle8 database. DB_VERIFY (also described in Chapter 3) will diagnose problems in the rare event that the database gets broken! Previously the only way to guarantee the data was by periodically exporting it.

Security

In Oracle's new vision of computing, users' PCs don't have hard disks; all data is retained on the database server. If the database is now going to be the repository for increasingly more data from many different sources, it's all the more critical that the database be secure. Both database software and design practices must be in place that will protect the integrity and the privacy of the data.

Many users like having data stored on their own hard disks and are suspicious of this new vision. They worry that their data will be less secure if it can't be stored on their own personal PCs. Is this really the case? Many users store confidential files on their PCs in the deluded belief that doing so is much more secure than putting them on a server. Others insist that their mailboxes must also reside on the good old "C" drive. They feel comforted by the fact that the data is physically close to them. These same users are shocked and disappointed when:

- Their PCs are stolen and there are no backups

- The hard disk fails, and the last backup is more than two months old

- Other users can come along, log on with a suitable network login, and gain full access to the PC's hard disk

Oracle8 does provide better security features than Oracle7. Password management has been greatly improved within Oracle8. Oracle now offers most of the features that most operating systems have had for years (with the obvious exception of Windows!)—for example:

- Account disablement after a specified number of failed attempts

- Password expiration and forced password changes

- Password history maintenance to prevent users from reusing previous passwords

- Complex password enforcement that forces users to choose passwords which cannot easily be guessed by potential intruders

Global user accounts are supported through *distributed security domains*. With these, users who are registered on one instance are authenticated to connect to other named instances within a security domain. This is useful for organizations with a mobile or fluid workforce.

More Manageable Data

We mentioned earlier that some users have been exceeding the limits of database size and have been demanding support for larger amounts of

data. Large data volumes generally imply huge tables which become difficult to manage. Backing up large tables or dropping or recreating indexes
on large tables can take a prohibitively long time. Even loading new data
into a humongous table can be very slow. In the past, designers of data
warehouses have tended to get around these limitations and increase
speed by partitioning large tables into lots of smaller tables and by
creating views that perform a UNION ALL set operation to merge these
tables together. Oracle8 now supports *partitioned tables* which are split
on a partition key and are stored separately, but which can be accessed
as a whole through partition transparency. Indexes can also be partitioned, where appropriate.

Another mechanism new to Oracle8 that helps keep data more manageable is the *index-only table*. This is exactly what its name suggests: a
table that has index blocks but no data blocks. Such tables are ideal for
lookup data when you simply need to verify that a value exists and is
therefore valid.

Chapter 4, *Oracle8's "Big" Features*, describes both partitioned tables and
index-only tables.

More Copies of Data

Oracle8 has considerably improved support for data replication. Gone is
Oracle7's kludge implementation using triggers. It has been replaced by
code in the Oracle kernel that is far more efficient and less prone to
errors. In addition, a new technology called *parallel propagation* allows
you to achieve data replication much more quickly. Parallel propagation
allows modified data on one node to be propagated to many other nodes
on the network simultaneously.

Oracle7 replication did not support any tables with LONG or LONG RAW
columns. In Oracle8, however, LOB data (the replacement for LONGs)
can be replicated (although BFILEs cannot). (We'll describe both LOBs
and BFILEs in the next section.)

More Ways to Represent Data

Oracle7 provided a fairly primitive set of scalar data types (CHAR,
NUMBER, VARCHAR, DATE, RAW, LONG). Oracle8 has significantly
enriched this set by offering a new type system that includes support for
data collections (traditionalists can think of them as repeating groups).

Within certain limitations, users can now define their own data types,
using a facility unsurprisingly called *abstract data types* (or *ADTs*). These

can be simple scalar types or more complex "records," such as an address which may contain five address lines, a state, and a zip code. The biggest limitation is that there appears to be no way to specify constraints as part of a type definition, so it isn't possible to do such things as enforce an ADT for positive non-zero integers. Later in this chapter we'll show a brief example of an abstract data type (see the section "The Type System").

Those of us who have long suffered the restrictions of longs (bad pun intended) will welcome the new datatypes *LOB* and *BFILE*. LOBs (large objects) and BFILEs (binary files) have few of the restrictions of longs, and can be manipulated from within PL/SQL using the new DBMS_LOB package. The main difference between the two new datatypes is that a LOB is stored within the database and is subject to the transactional control of the database. A BFILE resides outside the database and is therefore not subject to transactional control. We'll describe these datatypes in greater detail in Chapter 4.

NOTE   The name BFILE (binary file) is rather surprising since all files held on a computer or magnetic storage are essentially binary. What distinguishes these files is that they are external to the database and are pointed to from within the database. It must have been tempting to name them the X-files!

Oracle8 also no longer restricts us to scalar items (i.e., columns) within a table. Tables can contain variable arrays (known in Oracle8 parlance as *VARRAYs*) and *nested* (or *embedded) tables*. A VARRAY is an ordered set of built-in object types (we'll describe types under "Object Orientation" later) with implicit index variables. A nested table is a table which appears as a column of another table.

A new type of index is also available in Oracle8—the *reversed key index*. This feature reverses the bytes of the columns within an index, although not the columns. So, if we indexed on (LASTNAME, FIRSTNAME) the index entry for IAN STEVENSON would be NOSNEVETS\0NAI.[*] Chapter 3 discusses why you might want to use this feature.

The *view* is one feature that has traditionally been used to represent data in many different ways. If, like us, you've been frustrated in the past by Oracle's restrictions on which views can be updated via SQL,

---

[*] We've used the C language convention which shows a binary zero inside a string as "\0".

then you are going to love the new *INSTEAD OF triggers*, which allow you to specify INSERT, UPDATE, and DELETE processing for absolutely any view. As you will see from the examples in Chapter 3, we do mean *any* view!

Faster Access to Data

Oracle8 offers significant performance enhancements over its predecessor. Data warehouse applications, in particular, will benefit from the new *star join parallel bitmap* technology. With this feature, Oracle finds qualifying rows in a fact table using *bitmap indexes*, and, in a second pass or phase, joins them to the relevant rows in the dimension tables. With the use of parallel processing, this type of query becomes orders of magnitude faster.

At a simpler, but no less significant, level, Oracle has introduced a new access method known as an *index full scan* which reads index leaf blocks from beginning to end. Because this scan is committed to reading all of the index leaf blocks, it can use the read-ahead facility; in many cases, it will be faster than a full table scan. The longer the rows and the shorter the keys, the more likely it is that an index full scan will beat a full table scan. Where a table has been analyzed and an index is available with no nullable keys, the query optimizer may elect to use an index full scan in situations where it would previously have used a full table scan.

Oracle has also introduced a server-based *Advanced Queuing Facility* (Oracle/AQ), available through a new PL/SQL package called DBMS_AQ. This package provides a kind of messaging system between client and server and can achieve high throughput of transactions from clients since it allows them to simply queue a message rather than directly act on the database. Clearly this approach requires careful design to guarantee data and application integrity, but in principle it is akin to middleware with the middleman cut out!

Both database recovery and DML operations (for partitioned tables) have been parallelized in Oracle8 and can therefore take full advantage of Symmetric Multiprocessing (SMP) and Massively Parallel (MPP) hardware.

Towards Object Orientation

Oracle8 is the first step on Oracle Corporation's evolutionary path toward object orientation. In its present form, the new version is by no means complete, but it does point the way toward an object-oriented database

(OODBMS) which uses a relational database engine as its delivery mechanism. At this point in the Oracle8 life cycle, we don't believe that many projects will want to invest much effort in trying to leverage Oracle8's object support until it better supports the full object paradigm. (We'll explore the reasons why more fully in Chapter 5, *Objects*.) We suspect that most projects will wait for a more rounded implementation that removes many of the current restrictions.

The Type System

User-defined types are known formally as abstract data types (ADTs). They can be used in PL/SQL declarations in place of the built-in types (such as VARCHAR and NUMBER), and they can also be used in tables. You can even base an entire row definition on a type. Member functions can be called directly from SQL and are syntactically equivalent to column references. Unfortunately, as you will see in Chapter 5, the syntax used to reference ADTs means that the application program must have some awareness that ADTs are in use.

You can encapsulate structures within table definitions using VARRAYs, nested tables, and LOBs. We've introduced these datatypes briefly above, and we'll discuss them more fully in the following chapters.

One of the true object-oriented features available in Oracle8 is *methods*. These can be defined as part of the definition of the type on which they operate. Methods are written in PL/SQL, but they are different from stored procedures in several ways:

1. You can invoke a method by referencing it from any occurrence of the type.

2. Methods can access all attributes and methods of the type on which they operate.

The following SQL*Plus script gives an example of the declaration of a type containing a method (in this case, a *member function*), and the use of this function within PL/SQL:

```
CREATE OR REPLACE TYPE circle AS OBJECT {
    x_pos   NUMBER,
    y_pos   NUMBER,
    radius NUMBER,
    MEMBER FUNCTION area RETURN NUMBER);
};

CREATE OR REPLACE TYPE BODY circle
    MEMBER FUNCTION area RETURN NUMBER IS
    BEGIN
```

```
          return(3.1417*radius*radius);
      END;
  END;
  /

  DECLARE
     my_circle CIRCLE;
     area      NUMBER;
     radius    NUMBER;
  BEGIN
     my_circle := circle(2,3,4);
     area      := my_circle.area; -- references a member function
     radius    := my_circle.radius; -- references a stored number
     DBMS_OUTPUT.PUT_LINE ( 'A circle of radius '
        || to_char(radius) || 'has an area of '
        || to_char(area));
  END;
  /
```

Object Views

Object views are designed to allow object-oriented development tools to access purely relational data as if this data were persistent objects of arbitrary complexity. The program doesn't need to concern itself about how the data is stored in the underlying database, only with the structure with which the object is presented. Object views should help with the implementation of OO applications that run against a purely relational persistent data store, though their use demands the combination of C (or C++) and embedded (OCI) calls. This is not easy stuff to implement, although Oracle Corporation has provided a service called the Object Type Translator (OTT) to generate the C and C++ structure definitions which correspond to the ADTs. We'll describe this service in Chapter 5.

2

Methodologies for Oracle8

There are many different methodologies that can be applied to a computer-based application development project. These methods have been used with varying degrees of success over the years. In particular, they have been applied in various ways to relational database developments. These methods provide a variety of diagramming tools that let analysts and designers visualize the world they are modeling.

During the past few years we have witnessed the emergence of a number of new methods created specifically to support object-oriented analysis and design (OOAD). Originally, object orientation was regarded as a way to program using languages such as C++ and SmallTalk. It has grown to encompass much more than that original limited goal; now, object orientation can apply through all the phases of system development. Yet matching object-oriented programming techniques with a relational database structure is a challenge. It generally forces us to have to compromise one or the other.

When we look at development methods for Oracle8, we find ourselves in a bit of a quandary: Oracle8 is a hybrid product that is part relational and part object-oriented. So what type of method should we be using in an Oracle8 development? Has the change in underlying functionality been sufficiently radical that we need to completely rethink our entire approach to development projects? To be perfectly honest, there is no straightforward answer to this question, but in this chapter we'll examine some of the issues and make some suggestions.

Oracle8 and Traditional Methods

When should you continue to use traditional development methods, and when should you use an entirely new, object-oriented method?

Obviously, you can take an existing Oracle7 system and run it on Oracle8. Oracle has always strongly supported forward compatibility. Such a system would run as well on Oracle8 as it did on Oracle7, but it wouldn't be able to take advantage of the many new Oracle8 features. Taking the argument to the next level, it's also possible to develop a new application on Oracle8 that doesn't use any of the new features. For a project such as this (and we expect there to be quite a few), traditional methods of development are just as appropriate as they were in Oracle7.

When we start examining some of the features of Oracle8, we have to question some of the concepts of relational modeling—for example, normalization. Since the relational model was first conceived, the principle of normalization has been sacrosanct. As designers, we take it for granted that the logical data model from which we design should be in at least third normal form (3NF). But let's first remind ourselves about *first* normal form (1NF), which asserts that only atomic attribute values are allowed. All repeating groups must be removed and placed in a new (related) entity. Oracle8 introduces two concepts which seem to be alien to first normal form. These are *nested tables* and *VARRAYs*; both appear to encourage unnormalized data structures.

We strongly recommend that the logical data model produced in analysis stay in third normal form. A logical model (as the name implies) should not make any assumptions about the vehicle for its physical implementation. The decision about whether to employ a structure such as nested tables or VARRAYs should be design decisions. Under what conditions would we employ these structures? If a parent entity in the data model has a child that has a fixed number of rows and you are only interested in the child through the context of the parent, then it might be appropriate to implement the child table as a VARRAY. Figure 2-1 shows an example.

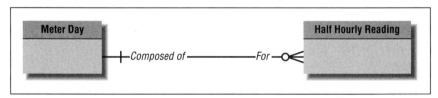

Figure 2-1: An entity-relationship diagram

In the United Kingdom's electricity industry, the day is divided up into 48 half-hour periods to allow the price of electricity to fluctuate depending on the time of day, as demand varies. In this case, we have a fixed number of readings from power meters which are billed on a half-hourly basis. The individual readings are only of significance within the day as a whole, so we create a VARRAY and situate them in the meter_days table as follows:

```
CREATE TYPE hh_reading AS VARRAY(48) OF NUMBER(9,2);
CREATE TABLE meter_days(reading_date,
    meter_status, hh_reading,…);
INSERT INTO meter_days VALUES (sysdate, 'OK',
    hh_reading(187263.23, 72653.98,…),…);
```

In our example, rest assured that we will never have to contemplate redimensioning the VARRAY—there will always be 48 half-hour periods in a day. This is an important factor since it's not trivial to do the redimensioning. We can also be confident that these readings are purely numbers. We know we won't want to find meters or meter days based on individual half-hourly readings. If it turned out that we wanted to look for meters with specific reading values, then we would have made a bad choice because a VARRAY cannot be indexed. The Half Hour Readings are physically stored with their Meter Day, so when we retrieve them for a given Meter Day, there is little or no additional I/O. It is a bit like clustered tables in that respect.

One massive restriction is that you cannot select individual elements of a VARRAY using SQL. You will have to consider this restriction as you make your overall design decision. It may or may not be a problem for you, depending on what programming languages/4GLs you're planning to use to extract the data.

Oracle8 and OOAD

As we will learn in Chapter 5, *Objects*, Oracle8 supports only a subset of what most object gurus would call full object orientation. As a result, we believe that at present, traditional methods are still the most appropriate to use. Remember that we are still building tables (not classes) for an underlying engine that is still largely relational. We recommend that at this point you regard object-oriented analysis and design (OOAD) tools as complementary to the traditional approach of entity modeling, process modeling, data flows, and other such concepts; they are not replacements for these traditional approaches.

In the analysis phase of a project we still need to identify entities, as we describe in Chapter 3 of our original book, *Oracle Design*. We might start calling these entities object classes, but they are largely the same thing. Object classes have attributes (as do entities); they also have methods. In a traditional method, we also identify a function hierarchy—that is, we break down the functional description of the system until we have atomic functions that cannot be broken down further. These functions are then cross-referenced to entities and attributes using a method called CRUD (Create, Read, Update, Delete) analysis for an entity in a function. OOAD is not like this; with OOAD, we identify *methods* that operate on the object classes and *messages* that are passed between the objects.

In an object model, the type or class diagram represents the model to probably a larger extent than the entity relationship model (ERM) does in a relational system. If we examine an example type/class diagram, shown in Figure 2-2, we should be able to see what distinguishes it from an ERM.

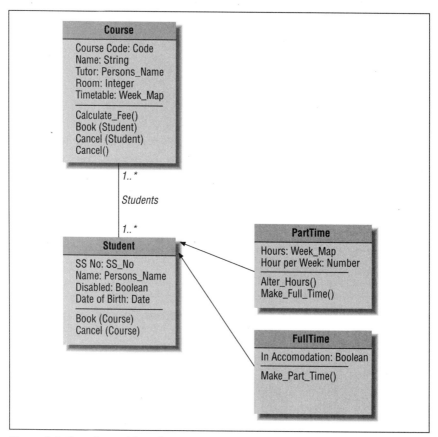

Figure 2-2: Sample type/class diagram

These are the major differences we can observe between the ERM and the corresponding type/class model:

- The diagram doesn't merely depict data; it also shows methods that are encapsulated in the data. For instance, it indicates that a method of Student is to book him or her in a course (passed as an argument). Interestingly, a method of Course is also to book a student; this is achieved by passing a student object as an argument.

- The data types are far more varied and complex than we would find in an entity relationship model. For instance, we have a type to hold a person's name that will probably include subtypes of a surname, given name, and title. This is more than can be achieved with traditional domains.

- This is only one view of the type model. The Tutor residing in a Course may well be an object in its own right. Classes can contain other classes. The Week Map (used to hold a list of hourly slots within a week) may also be a model. The Week Map is used to indicate the hours in a week that a part-time student attends, as well as the weekly timetable of a course. We would expect a method to be available that would be used to determine whether a part-time student could take a given course by "ANDing" the two Week Maps.

- PartTime and FullTime are subtypes of Student. They will inherit all properties and methods of Student and have additional ones of their own. One of the major activities involved in OOAD is the organization of hierarchies of classes. Unfortunately, Oracle8 does not support the principle of inheritance.

You can see from this type model that we can derive both the class structure and the persistent database design. The methods are encapsulated with their classes and would be implemented as encapsulated functions and procedures. Embedded or contained objects, such as our Tutor in the example, can be implemented as references. Our many-to-many relationship between Students and Courses is interesting. We could go down the relational route of introducing an intersection entity called "Course Booking". Alternatively, we could have a VARRAY of references to Courses in our Students object and a VARRAY of references for Students in Courses. In fact, this could be quite an interesting implementation as long as we can ensure that the two stay in sync.

This section introduces some of the concepts of object modeling. Of course, this is a massive subject in its own right and there are many good books on the subject. We didn't feel it was appropriate to delve too deeply into the subject when we're advocating that you don't use it. If you produce a lovely, pure OO model, you might be deeply disappointed when you find that you can't implement most of it in Oracle8!

Component-Based Development

Most systems in production today are designed as isolated, monolithic systems. These require significant reworking whenever a business practice or market force changes or whenever legislation requires a change. Such systems were conceived and designed with little or no thought about reuse of any part of the system. Throughout the world, the wheel is constantly being reinvented. Even within an organization, we witness the same problem being solved over and over in different applications.

Our vision of the future is that application development will undergo a significant change in the next few years. We believe the trend will be toward more component-based systems: You won't be building a complete system from scratch; rather, you will be seeking out components that will do the job for you, building your own functionality based on existing components (either developed in-house or bought from a third party), and providing the glue to bolt them together into an application system.

To some extent, this trend has already started, although until now it has been mostly focusing on client development tools. Microsoft Visual Basic has had this concept for several years now with VBX, OCX, and, most recently, ActiveX. There is no end of third-party controls available in the market today. Less common are server-based components. With the arrival of the Network Computing Architecture and the use of cartridges, Oracle is now encouraging developers to write components so the company can build up a significant portfolio of cartridges that it endorses. One significant advantage of a component-based project is the reduction in the testing effort required, since the components that you are building with are tried and tested—or, at the very least, you assume they are, which is not quite the same thing.

As components become more prevalent, the methods employed on development projects must evolve. We expect that analysis will still gather the requirements, but also will seek out appropriate component software and perform "gap" analysis. Such an analysis measures how closely the component(s) can deliver the required functionality.

You can view each component in terms of a set of object classes. One of the designers' functions in the brave new world will be to formulate a class hierarchy for the object classes. Suppose that we are going to deploy a low-level imaging class that has methods such as "scan," "store," "index," etc. We might create our own classes, such as "store document," that inherit properties from the base imaging classes. We might choose to insert a generic set of classes, such as "create new document," between the low-level classes and our high-level one.

How soon will we reach this pinnacle of component-based development? Well, it has actually already begun, and Oracle is running schemes such as competitions to encourage the interest of developers. One potential problem with component-based development is the lack of a universal language to code components. Many components will require interaction between cartridges on the client, on the database server, and possibly on the application server. Currently, NCA cartridges can only be developed in a mixture of C/C++ and PL/SQL. Once the Java revolution has really taken off, we will start to see extensible cartridges that slot into both the client and the server components.

Realistically, there will always be custom development work. Our vision of the future is not code-free applications. What we foresee is much more cross-licensing of relatively cheap stable technology that will take much of the donkeywork out of designing and coding application systems.

Bottom-Up or Top-Down Development

Some object experts would have you believe that OOAD takes a bottom-up approach; they analyze all the low-level objects (such as orders and customers) in an organization and start to design and develop properties and methods around those objects. Then they create a set of higher-level objects based on the original set, followed by another level, and so on. The theory is that when you want to build an application, you already have the majority of what you need and it is simply a case of bolting it together.

Nice theory! However, it falls down on several points:

- It would require an enormous amount of up-front development, with no specific application coming from this huge investment. Most financial controllers and budget-holders would want more tangible deliverables from their investment.

- Objects are unlikely to be well defined. For instance, the structure and behavior of an order is very different depending on whether it is viewed from the Sales Ledger System or the Order Processing System.

It is difficult to model an organization in a way that satisfies all the departments or components.

An alternative approach is a top-down model that is implemented using stubs for low-level classes that haven't yet been created. These lower-level classes are decomposed, and stubs are created for the next level of class until, finally, atomic classes are defined and developed.

3

Miscellaneous Oracle8 Enhancements

Chapter 4 and 5 describe the two major new categories of features in Oracle8—features supporting larger databases (Chapter 4, *Oracle8's "Big" Features*) and features supporting object orientation (Chapter 5, *Objects*). This chapter describes the Oracle8 features that don't fit into either of these categories but that do have an important impact on the design of Oracle databases and code.

INSTEAD OF Triggers

Oracle7 introduced the concept of database triggers that fired before or after a particular event (an INSERT, DELETE, or UPDATE) occurring on a table. These triggers could fire either at the row or the statement level, thus yielding a total of 12 events. Version 7.1 added the ability to have multiple triggers for the same event. This feature overcame a number of practical difficulties; the most obvious was that many different applications could now apply their own triggers to a particular event without having to be aware of the logic required by each other. Oracle designers have used triggers to great effect, particularly in the implementation of denormalization and the enforcement of complex data rules.

With the coming of Oracle8, many designers and developers had hoped that Oracle8 would support SELECT triggers. Such triggers would enable queries to be intercepted and would allow user-specified logic to take place at query time; simply recording the query would have been a major potential use of such a trigger. SELECT triggers would have also been a powerful tool in implementing auditing and data-sensitive security. But however appealing such SELECT triggers might be, they are not what INSTEAD OF triggers are about.

How INSTEAD OF Triggers Work

In Oracle8, there is something new in the world of triggers: INSTEAD OF triggers. These are triggers which are defined on a view rather than on a table. Such triggers can be used to overcome the restrictions placed by Oracle on any view which is deemed to be non-updatable. Prior to Version 7.3, it was impossible to issue DML (Data Manipulation Language) statements—INSERT, DELETE, and UPDATE—against any view which contained a join. In Version 7.3, it became possible to issue DML against a join view, but only with severe restrictions. Only columns belonging to one table can be updated in a single statement, and the view must be *key preserved*, meaning that the join key column(s) may not be updated.

In Oracle8, INSTEAD OF triggers are defined on the same events as their table counterparts: INSERT, DELETE, and UPDATE. Since there is no provision for a trigger which is run at lock time, then either locking must be implicit or the application must know what objects to lock (or from which tables to perform a SELECT...FOR UPDATE). Despite this minor inconvenience, the new triggers have removed a major constraint on design. The designer now has the ability to specify the logic to be used to perform DML against any view definition, and this logic need only be implemented once (in the triggers). Without these triggers, designers had two choices:

- The view update logic had to be placed in a stored procedure which every application that used the trigger was expected to call

- Worse, each application was expected to contain its own version of the logic

The problem with these solutions is that both of them are *cooperative*— that is, they work only if each application behaves according to the same set of rules. Cooperative solutions make maintenance somewhat daunting.

There are a few restrictions on INSTEAD OF triggers:

- They are available only at the row level, not at the statement level

- They can be applied only to views and not to tables

The second restriction raises a surprising anomaly if you issue this statement:

```
CREATE VIEW emp_view AS SELECT * FROM emp;
```

It would be legal to declare a trigger as follows:

```
CREATE TRIGGER emp_insert INSTEAD OF INSERT ON emp_view
BEGIN
```

```
    DELETE FROM emp
    WHERE empno = :new.empno;
END;
```

However, it would be illegal to declare the same trigger on emp even though the resulting action would be identical. The completely legal view shown in this definition is an example of *subversion*. Any normal maintenance programmer who knows or can inspect the view definition, and encounters the statement:

```
INSERT INTO emp_view (empno, ename, deptno)
    VALUES (1111, 'SMITH', 40);
```

will assume that the result of the statement (as long as no error occurs) will be at least one new row in emp. Conventional triggers may augment that action in any number of ways, but the basic meaning of the statement will still be reflected in the result.

The INSTEAD OF trigger carries no such guarantee. As our example shows, the result may be quite contrary to the apparent meaning of the statement invoking the trigger. Because the code is encapsulated in the trigger, unless you have access to the data dictionary and can both discover the existence of the trigger and inspect the trigger text, you will encounter an apparent mystery: you saw an insert being issued against emp_view, but when you retrieved from emp_view, your new data was nowhere to be seen! However, if the insert has resulted in a duplicate empno being added (or, more likely, a primary key violation) then the row currently containing that employee number will be deleted. The example may seem extreme, but we have tested it and it "works."

Use INSTEAD OF triggers *very* carefully. Avoid specifying what we call *naked subversion*—that is causing the server to silently avoid taking the precise action which any reasonably informed observer would predict. We also recommend against the use of multiple INSTEAD OF triggers firing at the same event on the same view. This is supported, but does not appear to us to be sensible. Why? By their nature, the triggers are independent and don't need knowledge of each others' actions, and yet they are specified as operating *instead of* the specified operation—rather than *as well as*—which is the case with other triggers,

There are, however, a number of cases in which INSTEAD OF triggers can be used with great effect. As we discussed in *Oracle Design*, views can be used to implement security restrictions by restricting certain groups of users to a subset of the data in a table. This subset might be a horizontal partition (restricting rows), a vertical partition (restricting columns), or both. The access to the table is controlled entirely through the view which traditionally could not be updated (unless the restrictions were implemented using subqueries rather than the joins). In addition, the INSTEAD OF triggers may be used to conditionally restrict certain operations or conditionally supply values to the table that aren't defined in the view.

Oracle Forms designers often used views of pre-join tables as the basis of a block, as an alternative to basing a block on one of the tables and making expensive post-query calls to the server. The problem with this solution was that the developer would have to develop a series of "ON-" triggers to override the default functionality provided by Oracle Forms. With INSTEAD OF triggers, the form need not be aware that it is operating against a view since the issuing of inserts, deletes, and updates is dealt with on the server.

WARNING   As we mentioned earlier, it is not possible to write a database trigger which fires at LOCK time, so although the view can be made updatable, there is no encapsulated way of requesting a lock on the set of rows from which any row in a view is derived. Thus, it is not possible to update such views from Oracle Forms under the default locking model. The only options within the Forms-level ON LOCK trigger are to explicitly lock the row, or simply not to lock them at all. Faced with that choice, we would elect not to lock rather than to have a series of assumptions about a view definition buried in a form.

A Trigger Example

To give some idea of just how much imagination the designer can employ in creating an INSTEAD OF trigger, consider a summary view which gives the total of all salaries by department:

```
CREATE VIEW totsal
       ( dname
       , sal_amount
       ) AS
SELECT d.dname
       , SUM(e.sal)
   FROM emp   e
       , dept d
  WHERE d.deptno = e.deptno
  GROUP BY d.dname;
```

Most people, when they are learning SQL, have little difficulty in understanding why this view cannot be updated. Let's assume, however, that we decide that when we allocate more money to a department's salary budget, we want that money to be shared equally among the employees. We create an INSTEAD OF trigger:

```
CREATE OR REPLACE TRIGGER deptsal_update
   INSTEAD OF UPDATE ON deptsal
DECLARE
   emps NUMBER;
   diff NUMBER;
   dno  NUMBER;
BEGIN
   IF :new.dname != :old.dname
   THEN
      UPDATE dept SET dname = :new.dname
               WHERE dname = :old.dname;
   END IF;
   IF :new.totsal != :old.totsal
   THEN BEGIN
-- get the department number
-- will get error if two depts have same name
      SELECT deptno INTO dno
        FROM dept
       WHERE dname = :new.dname;
-- get the number of employees in the department
-- will cause divide by 0 if dept does not exist
      SELECT COUNT(*) INTO emps
        FROM emp
       WHERE deptno = dno;
-- apply the salary change
      diff := (:new.totsal - :old.totsal) / emps;
      UPDATE emp
         SET sal = sal + diff
       WHERE deptno = dno;
   END;
   END IF;
END;
```

Using Oracle's standard DEPT and emp tables (and the usual 4 departments and 14 employees) plus the view and trigger described, the apparently meaningless statement:

```
UPDATE totsal
   SET dname = INITCAP(dname)
     , sal_amount = sal_amount + 6
 WHERE dname = 'SALES';
```

will add 1 to each salesperson's salary and also change the name of department 30 from "SALES" to "Sales." Trying to perform an INSERT or a DELETE against the view will simply give the error that the view cannot be updated, as in earlier versions of Oracle. Of course, we could have provided INSERT and DELETE triggers which added a new department (with no employees) and removed both the department and its employees. Now you might have a different view as to how the money should be shared out. You want to calculate the increase as a percentage of the total bill and to apply that percentage increase to each employee. Easy enough.

When we tested this example, we made sure that there was a foreign key constraint on the deptno column in the emp table, half expecting to encounter our old friend the *constraining and mutating table restriction.* We wrote about this restriction in *Oracle Design,* and many of you have told us that this information was of immediate use to you in your work. We are very pleased to have helped some of you overcome the problem of constraining and mutating tables, but we're even more pleased to report that this restriction did not appear while we were testing the example shown.

The Role of INSTEAD OF Triggers

The short examples in this section may seem a bit extreme, but they serve to make two points:

1. For *any* view, if you can define a meaning for INSERT, UPDATE, or DELETE then you can set out to implement the required actions.

2. Even if these actions make perfect sense to you, they may not be at all intuitive to anyone else, and they will be both encapsulated and potentially difficult to find. Using multiple INSTEAD OF triggers will only make this situation worse.

Unfortunately, we expect that some designers will overuse INSTEAD OF triggers and therefore cause serious damage to the maintainability, and possibly even the integrity, of their applications. Nevertheless, we do believe that INSTEAD OF views have a natural role in allowing INSERT, UPDATE, and DELETE to be applied to views which would otherwise not be updateable (at least in those cases where the rules for updating are not contentious). Examples of such cases include:

- Allowing updates to single-table views which for security reasons do not project a NOT NULL column which is present on the table.

- Join views which translate codes into their standard meaning: such views can be a source of major performance enhancement in client/ server operation. Again, UPDATE and DELETE triggers may make perfect sense.

- UNION ALL views used to support manual partitioning. In this case, it will often be quite simple to code trigger logic to determine which of the partitions is subject to any particular DML operation. However, remember that although manual partitioning allows key partitioning to be applied using any scheme the designer chooses to employ (rather than the restricted LESS THAN mechanism used by Oracle8's automatic partitioning), we would not normally expect performance benefits from the use of the view.

We regard INSTEAD of triggers as a useful addition to the designer's repertoire, but one we recommend you use only sparingly.

PL/SQL Improvements

Oracle's procedural language, PL/SQL, has improved steadily since it was first introduced. Oracle6 brought us PL/SQL running inside the server, and Oracle7 iced that cake with stored packages and procedures, as well as triggers. Oracle7 also introduced both records and tables. As users gained more experience with these features, however, they began to express a number of concerns about both efficiency and functionality. Tables, in particular, turned out to be rather awkward structures to manage and were somewhat unfairly associated with memory leaks.[*]

With Oracle8, PL/SQL has improved in a number of areas. New features have been added, and we have been told that there is also a more direct interface between the SQL and PL/SQL engines. In previous versions of Oracle, these two engines had been kept quite separate for ease of maintenance. Unfortunately, this separation caused additional execution overhead when one of the engines had to call the other.

PL/SQL is crucial for object support, and it provides a number of additional features as well. The new version of the language, PL/SQL8, offers these new facilities:

* Allows you to write methods for direct types
* Supports the declaration and manipulation of object types and collections
* Allows the calling of external functions and procedures
* Comes with new libraries of built-in packages

PL/SQL has been upgraded to support directly most of the new features of the DBMS but not partitioned objects. That is unfortunate because we think these objects are likely to be the feature of most immediate benefit to users with large databases. There is extensive support for the new type system and the support for tables has been much extended.

---

[*] Although the use of PL/SQL tables could cause a user's Oracle server process to grow continuously under Oracle7, this was due to published restrictions on the way in which PL/SQL tables had been implemented, and workarounds could be coded.

We have yet to prove conclusively that tables in PL/SQL8 have sufficient functionality and efficiency to be usable for holding application caches on the server, but our experiments to date have been encouraging.

The following new built-in packages are supported in PL/SQL8:

DBMS_AQ
> Interfaces to the Advanced Queuing Facility (Oracle/AQ).

DBMS_AQADM
> Performs administrative tasks for Oracle/AQ.

DBMS_LOB
> Manipulates large objects (LOBs). See the discussion in Chapter 4.

DBMS_ROWID
> Encapsulates information about the ROWID datatype structure and allows ROWID conversion.

For a thorough exploration of PL/SQL, including the latest Oracle8 features, see the second edition of Steven Feuerstein's very popular book, *Oracle PL/SQL Programming*.

3GL Callouts

Many server applications need to be able to perform functions which are either awkward or inefficient in PL/SQL (such as parsing a command string) or totally impossible (such as navigating a local directory structure). Oracle has provided a few built-in packages, such as DBMS_FILE, to enable PL/SQL to communicate with the outside world, but their offerings in this area have generally been sparse and lacking in functionality and robustness.

As we mentioned in the previous section, a number of detailed improvements have been made to PL/SQL during the transition to Oracle8; these may reduce the number of cases under which it is necessary (or highly desirable) to call out to a 3GL routine. However, as welcome as these improvements are, they certainly will not eliminate the absolute requirement to be able to call 3GL code in a number of cases for both functional and efficiency reasons. In this context, "efficiency" includes not only runtime efficiency but also development efficiency. If the logic you need already exists as a fully tested and operational C function, then to rewrite it in PL/SQL is an unwanted expense. Having to maintain two versions of the same logic in different languages for the next five years is even more unwanted and potentially even more expensive.

With Version 7.3 there are two principal design options when you need a callout to a 3GL routine:

- Use one or more listener processes and communicate with them through the DBMS_PIPE package

- Send and receive messages to and from Network Computer Architecture (NCA) cartridges

We have little direct experience with the NCA, but we have used the pipe technique with some success. Note, though, that as the pipe traffic increases, a number of unwanted delays can occur. Both techniques involve message passing which is excellent from an object viewpoint but which the poor struggling program author may consider to be overkill. Both techniques require robust control mechanisms to ensure that the appropriate pipe listener or service cartridges are up and running. Inevitably, both solutions increase the systems administration load.

The result has been many, many requests to Oracle for callouts from SQL (or PL/SQL) to 3GL routines resident on the server. This feature is present in Oracle8. If you cannot find it in any manual, this is probably because in the manual set Oracle refers to the feature as *external procedures*. The call to the 3GL must be made from PL/SQL (rather than SQL) For more information on the mechanism, see Oracle's *PL/SQL User's Guide and Reference* and the new edition of Steven Feuerstein's book.

TIP   The lack of a direct 3GL interface from SQL is a minor issue since it is possible to embed calls to PL/SQL functions within a SQL statement and these functions can in turn call an external procedure.

Restrictions on 3GL Callouts

There are a number of key restrictions on the callout support. Perhaps the most significant are the following:

- C is the only language supported

- The call must be from a dedicated server, not a multi-threaded server (MTS)

- The 3GL routine runs in a separate process (*extproc*) from the Oracle server

The first restriction is very minor if you are a C programmer, and is only a minor nuisance if you are a C++ programmer. (C++ and C are sufficiently similar that you already have the knowledge to write the required interface routine.) However, this restriction can be a major hurdle if you want to write in any other language since you will need to learn enough C to create an interface layer.

NOTE   Oracle has announced that Version 8.1 will directly support Java as a language for external procedures.

The second restriction is clearly a terminal problem if you must use MTS, and is of no concern if you do not.

The third restriction is much more severe and means that you will incur a minimum of two server-level context switches each time you call an external routine. On every current operating system we're familiar with, this can become a significant performance issue. It means, in effect, that callouts must be restricted to handling significant events rather than being used to support predicate clauses in full table scans.

TIP   In cases where a 3GL routine is needed to calculate a value, and that value is frequently required during query operations, we normally advise that the value be calculated at insert and update time and be stored with the record to which it refers. The clear exception to this advice is when there are frequent updates to other tables which change the derived value. Note that our recommendation here is the same as it was for Oracle7.

Example of a 3GL Callout

In Figure 3-1, we show the execution path of a query which calls a 3GL written in COBOL, and in turn uses the callback feature to issue SQL in the same context as the calling application. This example is based on a large car rental application where the pricing algorithm used several megabytes of private cache for efficiency reasons. Under Oracle7, communication with the 3GL routine was handled using the DBMS_PIPE package.

Traditional 3GLs are classified as "unsafe" because they have the ability to interrogate and change any unprotected memory location. If you are running within an Oracle server process, you have the ability to corrupt

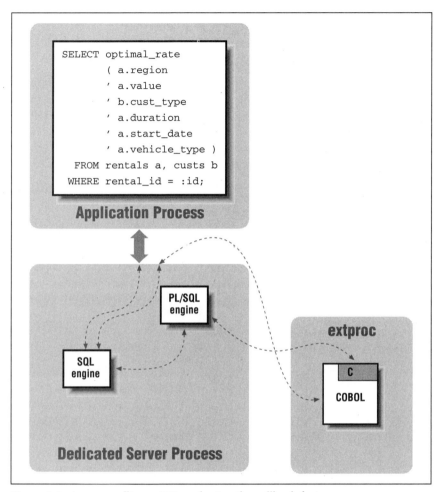

```
SELECT optimal_rate
        ( a.region
        ' a.value
        ' b.cust_type
        ' a.duration
        ' a.start_date
        ' a.vehicle_type )
   FROM rentals a, custs b
  WHERE rental_id = :id;
```

Application Process

PL/SQL engine

extproc

SQL engine

C

COBOL

Dedicated Server Process

Figure 3-1: A query calling a 3GL and using the callback feature

the System Global Area (SGA) on which Oracle depends absolutely for correct database operation. Java, on the other hand, is classified as a "safe" language (since it is interpreted and runs within the protection of the Java Virtual Machine). Oracle has stated that external procedures will run within the Oracle server process in Version 8.1. In other words, Java execution (complete with J/SQL for executing SQL statements) will then become a service provided by the Oracle server. The effect will be to change the situation shown in Figure 3-1 to the potentially more efficient one shown in Figure 3-2.

Whether this approach is actually more efficient will depend on whether the gains achieved by operating within the Oracle server process, and avoiding the context switches, fully compensate for any loss of efficiency

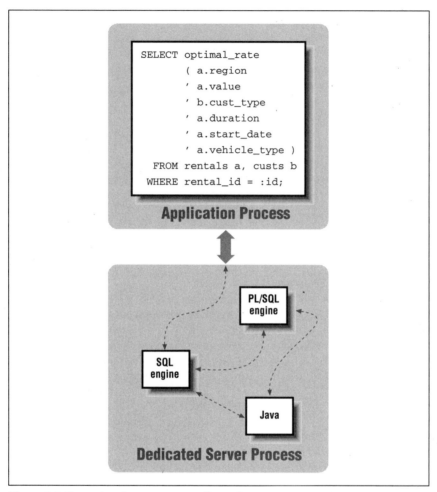

```
SELECT optimal_rate
           ( a.region
           ' a.value
           ' b.cust_type
           ' a.duration
           ' a.start_date
           ' a.vehicle_type )
     FROM rentals a, custs b
   WHERE rental_id = :id;
```

Application Process

PL/SQL engine

SQL engine

Java

Dedicated Server Process

Figure 3-2: Executing the query more efficiently

incurred through using Java. Certainly, very few of the several billion lines of legacy code on this planet are currently available in Java, so if you are hoping to take advantage of 3GL callouts to reuse existing service routines, then waiting for Java support in Version 8.1 is not going to help very much.

Deferred Constraint Checking

In our earlier book, we devoted an entire chapter to entity relationship modeling. We explored implementation options in Oracle for various constructs that can occur in a model. Our philosophy has always been that we prefer to enforce constraints and conditions arising from the model in the server and to use Oracle-provided facilities such as constraints wherever possible. What has caused us some grief, however, is the enforcement of relationships that are mandatory at both ends. Consider the example shown in Figure 3-3.

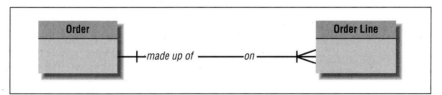

Figure 3-3: A relationship that is mandatory at both ends

In this model, we assert that we cannot have an order line unless we have the corresponding order (which is fair enough), but we also assert that we don't allow orders which have no lines. The problem is that we have to violate one of these rules temporarily since we can't create the Order and its first Order Line simultaneously. We don't really care about this temporary violation as long as it is rectified by the time we come to commit.

To enforce the rule that an Order Line must be on an Order, we could define a foreign key constraint on the Order_Lines table and make the foreign key columns NOT NULL. To enforce the assertion that an Order must have at least one Order Line, we could write a row-level trigger on Orders that fired on insert, update, and delete, and check for Order Lines. Now we have a classic chicken and egg scenario. If we attempt to create the Order first, then the trigger will fail the transaction, if we attempt to create the Order Line first, then the constraint will fail it.

However, if we create the constraint as *deferrable*, then Oracle8 can leave its checking until the transaction is committed, at which point it will be satisfied since the Order will have been created. Deferred constraint checking is exactly what it says: it can be used to defer the checking of constraints but it cannot be used to defer trigger execution. In our example above, some might argue that although we have broken the chicken and egg circle, we've broken it the wrong way because it would be more logical to create the Order first. We disagree with this view. To us, the only truly logical approach is to create the Order and its Order Lines simultaneously, an action which is simulated in Oracle and other environments using COMMIT and ROLLBACK statements.

NOTE   As you will see in Chapter 5, where we discuss Oracle8 ob-
                ject support, it is entirely possible in Oracle8 to arrive at a
                schema which would allow (and possibly require) a single
                SQL INSERT statement to create both a new order and all
                of its order lines. However, just because something is possi-
                ble does not mean that it is a good idea.

To support deferred checking of constraints, each constraint has two additional attributes:

- It may be deferrable or not deferrable

- It may be initially deferred or initially immediate

Thus, the following statement:

```
ALTER TABLE emp ADD CONSTRAINT emp_dept_check
    FOREIGN KEY deptno REFERENCES dept
    DEFERRABLE INITIALLY DEFERRED;
```

will add a constraint which will by default only be checked at commit
time. The constraint, and the fact that it is checked at commit time, are
both *encapsulated* within the definition of the table emp. A user with
enough knowledge of the data dictionary can find out that the deferred
constraint exists, but code which manipulates the emp table does not
need to know about the existence of this feature. From a design viewpoint, therefore, we were a little concerned to see that Oracle8 allows
applications to issue SQL of the form:

```
SET CONSTRAINTS emp_dept_check IMMEDIATE;
```

This is SQL-92 syntax and it may well be that support for it was included
simply to be in accordance with the standard. However, we think that
application code has enough problems without having to know the
names of the constraints which have been applied to the tables they are
manipulating. We do not encourage the use of this option. We prefer the
alternative forms:

```
SET CONSTRAINTS ALL IMMEDIATE;
```

and

```
SET CONSTRAINTS ALL DEFERRED;
```

However, there is a minor design trap in these forms since some of the
constraint checking which is required within the transaction may be
marked as not deferrable. SET CONSTRAINTS lasts for the duration of the
transaction, but neither it nor subsequent statements issue warnings if the

action which it is being asked to take cannot be applied because one (or all) of the constraints encountered is not deferrable.

WARNING   We advise you to use deferred constraint checking only when absolutely necessary. If at all possible, avoid referencing constraint names within the application. If you think that deferred checking of referential integrity may solve a design problem, be aware that very few application programs cope well with commit time errors. Under previous versions of Oracle these were extremely rare.

ENFORCE Option

In *Oracle Design*, we devoted an entire chapter to the trials and tribulations of data migration and data take-on. In our work on these projects, we've observed a tendency by management to migrate data, "warts and all," to avoid a potentially time-consuming data clean-up exercise. Having carefully designed our database with constraints and triggers to protect the integrity of our data, we are instructed to remove them so the doors are now open to dirty legacy data. We are always assured that the data will be repaired when there is time. Of course there never is time!

With triggers that enforce data and integrity rules, we have always been able to "lock the door after the horse has bolted" and enable them after the data is loaded. This won't correct the incumbent data, but it prevents the problem from being proliferated with new data. With constraints, however, this was not the case in Oracle7—you could not enable a constraint on a table as long as there was data in the table that violated it. This meant that often the constraints were never enabled.

Oracle8 has an option to enforce a constraint rather than enable it. Enforcement is applied to any future inserts and updates, but does not care about data already in the table. The syntax is the following:

```
ALTER TABLE my_tab ENFORCE CONSTRAINT mt_cc1;
```

This option can also be very useful when enabling a constraint on a very large table since it avoids the considerable effort of having to check every row.

Safeguarding Data

Our earlier book dedicated an entire chapter to various mechanisms for protecting the data in your database. That chapter looked at subjects such as audit, security, and backup/recovery. We are pleased to observe that Oracle has made several enhancements in this area in Oracle8. This section describes these enhancements.

DB_VERIFY Utility

Oracle Design explored backup strategies for an Oracle database. In our discussion there, we noted that although backup is a DBA task, the designer of the database has knowledge about the placement and structure of the data and is often better informed than the DBA to formulate the policy for backup. We also noted that an image backup of the database files is the quickest means of backup. However, since an image backup copies a whole file, there is no guarantee of the integrity of the Oracle blocks within those files; you could be backing up corrupt or damaged files or overwriting good ones as you recycle your media. In Oracle7, one way to minimize the risk was to schedule periodic full database exports which trawl through the entire database structure. Doing this ensures its integrity (or alerts you to any problems). The main problem with full database exports is that they take a long time to run, especially on large databases.

Fear no more. Oracle8 includes a new utility called *DB_VERIFY* that can run either against an online database (or part of a database) or against a backup file or file set. This utility can also be used to help diagnose data corruption problems. DB_VERIFY is a handy weapon in the DBA's armory and should form an integral part of any backup strategy. We suggest that you use DB_VERIFY to check all backup files before cataloging them as part of the backup cycle. Although DB_VERIFY is the tool of choice when you suspect that there is a problem, we don't think the utility has much of a place in scheduled processing against a live database.

Recovery Manager Utility

Have you ever noticed how harassed the typical DBA looks? The DBA is in a no win situation and, in our opinion, is entitled to go gray prematurely. Database administration is a good deal like sports officiating. If you go to a sports event and don't notice the officials, then they had a good game; the only official who sticks in your mind is the one who made a dreadful decision. Similarly, when a database is humming along smoothly, nobody takes any notice of the DBA; he is just a faceless entity who monitors the database and adds new users when requested. However, when the database goes down or has problems, everyone (and we mean everyone) starts a witch hunt for the DBA. One of the authors was once a DBA and had the experience of trying to recover a database with a harassed operations manager watching over his shoulder, asking every five minutes how much longer it will take. Nobody needs this kind of pressure! Restoring a database isn't something you practice every day and when you do a restore, it's all too easy to panic and do something stupid.

Oracle Corporation has recognized that backing up, restoring, and recovering a database weren't easy tasks in Oracle7. In Oracle8, they have provided a tool to not only make the task easier, but also to automate it to a certain degree. This tool is the *Recovery Manager*.

The Recovery Manager runs as an agent process on the server. It initiates processes that back up or restore to a single database (the target database in Recovery Manager terms). It has its own scripting language, called the *Command Language Interpreter (CLI)*, so you can code scripts to automate your backups and restores. CLI can be typed in to an interpreter manually (through svrmgr) or can be run in batch by the Recovery Manager agent process. Here is a small sample of CLI that recovers a single tablespace with the database open:

```
run {
# script to recover the "users" tablespace while the database
# remains open
allocate channel dev1 type disk;
sql "alter tablespace users offline immediate";
restore tablespace users;
recover tablespace users;
sql "alter tablespace users online";
release channel dev1;}
```

Using the Recovery Catalog

The CLI scripts we mentioned in the previous section are held in the Recovery Catalog; that catalog holds all the useful information that the Recovery Manager requires to do its job. Oddly, the catalog resides in a database. We feel that this is poor design on Oracle's part and cannot fathom why it isn't held in a flat file. Clearly you can't store the Recovery Catalog in the target database because this way, if you lose the database, you also lose the thing that is supposed to help you to recover it. So, you need to have a second database. Oracle Corporation doesn't recommend your setting up a miniscule database with the sole purpose of housing the Recovery Catalog. Instead, they advise you to put it in a development, test, or support database. That's all very well if you have one and if it's on the same machine or accessible from the live environment!

The Recovery Manager must be periodically re-synced with the control file of the target database, so to use Recovery Manager effectively, you must have the catalog available most of the time. This somewhat limits your use of the database which contains the Recovery Catalog; you can't really bring the database down for too long. Also, because the Recovery Catalog is in a database, it must itself be backed up. Oracle suggests reversing the roles to achieve this, putting a Recovery Catalog in the production environment for the database that contains its catalog. Confused? We hope Figure 3-4 makes it clearer.

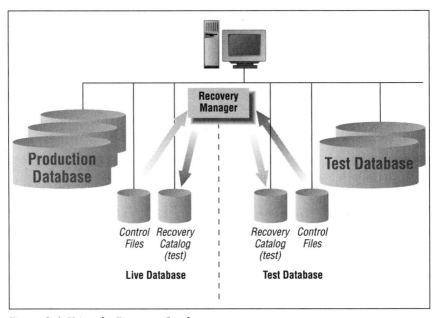

Figure 3-4: Using the Recovery Catalog

We acknowledge that this scheme is extremely convoluted, but given the fact that Recovery Catalogs must reside in databases, we can't come up with a more elegant solution. (Let us know if you do...) It is our belief that both databases must be Oracle8 in this scenario, but we haven't yet been able to confirm it.

Recovery Manager features

The following list summarizes many of the benefits of using the Recovery Manager:

- You can be very selective about what you back up. You can select a single tablespace or a named list of tablespaces for backup. There are options to skip any offline tablespaces and to skip "read-only" tablespaces (which should only require a single backup in their life-time).

- You can back up directly to tape, thereby avoiding having to reserve large amounts of disk for transient storage.

- Archived redo logs (or just plain logs as they are generally called) can be moved to tape through Recovery Manager commands. The logs can be selected on the basis of those whose data span a range of dates and times or by log sequence number.

- Recovery Manager supports point-in-time recovery.

- Recovery Manager has a series of reports and can generate lists of useful information about your backups.

- The various data files belonging to the database can be copied through the Recovery Manager.

- Incremental backup is now a feature. With previous versions of Oracle, the closest you could get to incremental backup was incremental exports. Unfortunately, the level of granularity of these was a table, so if the table had changed in any way since the last "incremental" export, then it would have to be exported again. Incremental exports were a good example of the chocolate teapot syndrome discussed in *Oracle Design.*[*]

- Incremental backups, on the other hand only take blocks that have changed since the time of the last backup. This very welcome feature could considerably reduce backup time for large tables that are subject to small levels of change.

- A checksum may be stored with each block that is backed up. Checksums can be verified on restore and will help safeguard against any file corruption.

TIP   Incremental backups are fine as long as the structure of
                 the database files being backed up hasn't changed. But be
                 sure to do a full backup if you add or remove a file or ta-
                 blespace

Recovery Manager is a very powerful and flexible tool. However, it is not an excuse to be sloppy. The designer must shoulder the responsibility of

---

[*] There is an old English saying, "as much use as a chocolate teapot," which means, of course, that it is of no use at all.

carefully planning the backup cycles for a system. Several important factors need to be juggled in formulating this strategy; among these are:

- The amount of time that the database or individual tablespaces can be offline for backup (if any)

- The amount of rollback segment required when backing up large online tablespaces

- The relative importance of the loss of data or the need to re-key data

- The time taken to recover a database (should the unthinkable ever happen)

- The spare capacity of disk on the system

An ad hoc strategy of backing up a tablespace here and a log file there will simply not suffice.

WARNING   Theoretically, you could probably get away with an ad hoc approach since Recovery Manager keeps internal track of what actions you perform, and it can guide you through recovery in the light of this knowledge. This tracking is vital for success; you must not do anything outside of Recovery Manager, such as take operating system copies of files. If you do, then you must use the *catalog* command to inform the Recovery Manager or you will be writing your own recipe for disaster.

4

Oracle8's "Big" Features

Some users of Oracle7 have found that they have been hitting the system's capacity limits in terms of both database size and the number of concurrent users that it can support. This has been particularly true of some of the large data warehouses that are using Oracle. To deal with their capacity problems, users have had to split their data and partition it between several databases—which is not an ideal solution. Oracle8 has introduced new levels of scalability that will address many of these capacity problems.

What Is a Really Big Database?

With the changes to the internal database structure in Oracle8, databases can now be quite trivially beyond the current practical limit of 2 terabytes. All you need is enough disk storage, data, and patience. Indeed, Oracle Corporation is now trying to persuade us to measure maximum database size in petabytes. A petabyte is 1,000 terabytes or 1,000,000,000,000,000 bytes. We're not trying to imitate *The Hitchhikers' Guide* (though we do both admire it), but we do have to point out that a petabyte is *really* big. Even just a terabyte (1,000,000,000,000 bytes) is a lot of data, but it is certainly not an unlimited amount of data. For example, a population tracking system using 4 kilobytes to track each of 250 million people would be (and perhaps already is) 1 terabyte in size. There are Oracle7 applications in production use that are already supporting in excess of a terabyte. To make these applications work, the sites have to use a variety of special techniques, such as segmenting the data across a number of physical databases. The "big" support in Oracle8 has two goals: to make such applications markedly less stressful to run than they currently are, and to reduce the amount of specialized application code required to handle these applications.

What about Oracle's limit on the number of users? Oracle has also performed early benchmarks on beta versions which have demonstrated support for 15,000 concurrent users. Awesome! And quite definitely "big."

The term "big" does not refer only to the size of the database. It encompasses the potential number of simultaneous users, the size of the total user community, and the size of the objects and attributes that can be stored in (or, as we shall see, out of) the database. It also encompasses operational considerations. The reference to the stress involved in trying to back up—or, worse still, restore—a 1-billion row table is another clue to how we define whether or not a database is really big. The criterion is simple: if size alone requires the designer to take some special action in order for the enterprise to cope with the application, then it is big.

We've come up with the following guidelines for an Oracle7 environment (though we don't necessarily expect Oracle Corporation to agree with our threshold figures):

1. Any column longer than a few megabytes is really big because it has to be inserted in one piece. In a system with many users, memory management and paging problems quickly occur because of the need for each user to hold in memory values that are several megabytes long. The design solution has been to decompose "values" such as video images into many chunks, each of a more manageable size.

2. Even without long columns, any column or row longer than the size of a database block size is really big. This is a consequence of the features of the storage allocator which require it to be decomposed for effective storage management.

3. Any application with more than 1,500 simultaneous users is big because it cannot reasonably be supported with a single instance if there is one physical database connection per user.

4. Any table is really big when the time needed to restore or index the table is greater than the time during which the enterprise is prepared to operate without access to the table.

5. Even if infinite time is available for restore and indexing, any table or index is really, really big when it cannot physically fit in the largest possible table space.

This chapter examines the Oracle8 embedded features that will allow your database to grow really big and will remove the need to create special, complex, and expensive project code simply to support the size. In many cases, using Oracle8 design and DBA features correctly is all you need to do to support really big applications and databases. We hope that Oracle8 will also further push the limit at which a project strays into the big domain. They've already made some moves in this direction. For example, Oracle8 has raised the limit on the number of columns per table (from 254 to 1,000). In the past, some projects have had to either use two rows to store a single record, or combine logically separate attributes into a single column. Now, such projects can simply define a table with the number of columns they want.[*]

Partitioned Objects

Any object which has been arbitrarily split up into pieces is said to be *partitioned*. The main reason that designers want to partition data is to make the data more manageable. The most common form of partitioning is *horizontal partitioning*, where a number of sets of rows are placed in separate containers; the Oracle8 support for partitioning supports this model, which does not require any duplication of data. The other form of partitioning, more rarely employed, is *vertical partitioning*, where two or more sets of columns are held in separate tables with the primary key of each row replicated in each table.

Partitioned Tables

The support for large tables in Oracle7 is not too bad. There are many data warehouses in production now with single tables containing several hundred gigabytes. If these tables are supported by a sensible index policy, then there is no reason why they should cause performance problems during normal operation. However, such tables may become somewhat unwieldy for administrative and recovery tasks. For instance, the tablespace containing the table will typically take a long time to back up, and because a table can't span tablespaces in Oracle7, the backup is all or nothing. Large tables are often subject to a heavy load of (yet more)

---

[*] If we were wearing our formal information theory hats, we'd have to spend the next five pages trying to demonstrate that no valid analysis is ever going to come up with entities having more than 254 attributes. However, we are aware that a small but significant number of projects actually do have such requirements—or at least have convinced themselves that they do, which is much the same thing.

data; if the mechanism for loading data uses the SQL*Loader direct path option, the table can't be used while it is being updated.

Administrative problems such as these have led designers of data warehouses to partition large fact tables. In Oracle7, they do this by designing a series of smaller tables, usually partitioned by date. For instance, consider a telephone company example: instead of designing a single table to record all calls made by customers, there would be a CALLS table for each month—CALLS_9801, CALLS_9802, etc. When an application requires a consolidated picture of the data, it accesses the tables through a view which performs a UNION ALL on the individual tables. This technique works quite well for queries; unfortunately, updating cannot be performed directly through the view, and the application has to be careful to ensure that DML takes place against the correct partition. For applications other than data warehouses, the implications of this manual partitioning are less acceptable. Figure 4-1 illustrates the example:

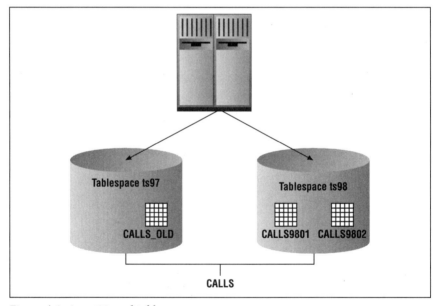

Figure 4-1: A partitioned table

When you start joining several hundred or, in some cases, several thousand, tables in a UNION ALL view, the parse time and memory requirements to execute the query can become a significant limiting factor. If only a few dozen summary reporting queries need to be issued each hour, this overhead isn't a major problem, but if tens of operational queries per second have to be satisfied, then you can't ignore parse times measured in seconds. Note, however, that if the query uses bind variables, it may be possible for Oracle to automatically cache it within the shared pool, thus avoiding the need for frequent parses.

Index lookup overhead may also become an issue. An ad hoc reporting query against a UNION ALL view or a partition view of 1,000 tables may well be supported via an index on each of the base tables referenced in the view. However, even with Oracle's manual partitioning support, the query processor will have to visit all 1,000 indexes in order to satisfy the query. Why? Because there is no mechanism for letting the optimizer know how the data has been partitioned. Of course we expect index root blocks to be memory-resident within the buffer cache. In many cases, you'll be able to determine from the index root block alone that a particular table contains no qualifying rows. Again in the case of a typical data warehouse query, an additional 1,000 index root block references are unlikely to have a major effect on the overall application performance. On the other hand, in a high-performance transaction processing system, they are likely to prove disastrous.

Declarative partitioning

Oracle8 provides a better solution to the partitioning of tables than anything available in Oracle7. It allows a single logical table to be split into many physically separate pieces based on ranges of key values. Each of the parts of the table is called a partition. Although the partitions are held and managed independently, they can be queried and updated by reference to the name of the logical table (or through a synonym or view which refers to that table name). In other words, Oracle8 provides *partition transparency*. The application doesn't require knowledge that the table has been partitioned.

Oracle8 also provides *partition independence*. With some restrictions which we'll discuss later under "Partitioned Indexes," you can access and manipulate data in one partition even if some or all of the other partitions are unavailable. This is a major benefit to administrators and users alike; it means that they can perform maintenance operations in a piecemeal fashion against individual partitions while the rest of the data remains available for use.

The same manual partitioning techniques available for Oracle7 are still available under Oracle8, and there is one major improvement. Oracle8 has INSTEAD OF triggers, which allow you to make the UNION ALL or partition view into an updateable object. At this point, we see little reason for you to use manual partitioning for new applications which will run only under Oracle8 unless you find the restrictions on partitioned tables

Transaction Processing

For many years we've expected transaction processing to be described by the acronym OLTP (online transaction processing). In fact, much of the Oracle8 documentation we've seen still makes many references to the differences between decision support applications and OLTP applications. You might notice that we've opted instead to use just the phrase transaction processing (without restricting these transactions to being *online*). Why is that?

Traditionally, massive batch updates, such as those associated with credit card and check clearing, have been performed in batch by mainframe systems; this approach is finally starting to change. As we go to press, a number of major financial organizations are performing their bulk processing using Oracle7; we expect this number to accelerate as Oracle8 moves into production. But whether such large applications are run on a traditional mainframe, a UNIX mainframe, or a Windows NT mainframe, we still expect that the main posting runs will continue to be performed in batch jobs. Batch processing improves performance and eases the problems of both audit requirements and failure recovery.

It's true that Web-based commerce might eventually push bulk applications to becoming fully online, and that their transaction processing load might then become OLTP. For the time being, however, we confidently predict a continuing role for the types of batch processes that have to wind their way through several million transactions once every 24 hours. Nothing we've seen in Oracle8 so far has fundamentally changed our traditional recommendations (described in Chapter 20 of *Oracle Design*) regarding the design of large-scale batch processing. Nevertheless, the improved support in Oracle8 for very large data populations makes it much more feasible to consider using Oracle as the data repository for populations of several billion transactions.

unacceptable—for example, if the partitions must be distributed across more than one physical database.

In our earlier example of recording telephone calls, automatic partitioning is most likely to be not only acceptable, but also highly desirable. We can encompass our partitioning approach within the table creation script:

```
CREATE TABLE calls
    ( call_from     NUMBER(12)
    , call_to       NUMBER(18)
    , call_start    DATE
    , call_seconds  NUMBER(6)
```

```
-- prefixing primary key with partition key is a good practice
, PRIMARY_KEY (call_start, call_from)
)
STORAGE (INITIAL 1000M NEXT 100M) LOGGING
PARTITION BY RANGE (call_start)
  ( PARTITION calls_old VALUES LESS THAN ('01-JAN-98')
     TABLESPACE ts97
  , PARTITION calls9801 VALUES LESS THAN ('01-FEB-98')
     TABLESPACE ts98
  , PARTITION calls9802 VALUES LESS THAN ('01-MAR-98')
     TABLESPACE ts98
  );
```

Any calls for January 1998 that are inserted into the CALLS table will automatically be placed in the CALLS9801 partition. Further, we can take some of the table partitions offline—for instance, to load some additional data or to perform a backup, and we can still continue to access the rest of the partitions through the table name.

WARNING   Our readers who have been battling with a Year 2000 project may be horrified to see two-digit years in the example. We have an admission to make:

Dave coded it the lazy way simply to make it easier to read. At least in the beta version, the form shown in our examples and the examples in the Oracle manuals does *not* work correctly for 21st century dates. Naturally, in the world outside this book, designers must require all date values to be specified using a TO_DATE function with a four-digit year or insist on the use of an RR mask for the year in the NLS_DATE_FORMAT initialization parameter.

But at least what we have reads nicely—which isn't always the case. As we observe in Chapter 5, *Objects*, one of the problems with using some of the new features in Oracle8 is that it becomes difficult, if not impossible, to quickly determine exactly what will happen from a scan of the SQL.

Partitioning a very large table offers a whole set of advantages, and Oracle8 allows partition transparency within almost the entire application. Only those parts of the application that deal with bulk deletion need to be aware of the partitions. However, when you are selecting a partition strategy, a number of key issues arise; the pun is intentional since most of these issues concern the partition key.

Selecting a partition strategy

The first rule of partitioning is this: never partition a table unless you have a good reason. There are two primary reasons—disk space and processing time. Building a 1 billion row table takes a great deal of both time and space. Then, if you need to delete 10 million rows from that table, the row deletion and associated index maintenance will also take a great deal of time; it may even require you to take the entire table out of production use. By partitioning the table, you reduce the size of your unit of failure from the size of the table to the size of your largest partition.

Oracle8 partition support is also the only mechanism built into the server that enables parallel update and delete operations. Suppose that we lose interest in calls to 800 numbers, and we issue a set operation such as this one:

```
DELETE FROM CALLS
    WHERE call_to BETWEEN 8000000000 AND 8009999999;
```

Oracle8 can parallelize this operation by starting a number of threads, each of which handles a single partition at a time. For implementation reasons, Oracle8 requires a parallel UPDATE or DELETE to be the only statement in the transaction. Thus, for these parallel operations to be of real use to you, you must have an application whose transactions:

- Perform large, set-based updates or deletes, and

- Do not need to touch any other table within the transaction

We don't think many real-world applications are likely to meet these criteria. As a result, we're going to continue to recommend that you parallelize bulk processing via application code (as we describe in Chapter 14 of *Oracle Design*). Bulk deletes are perhaps more likely to meet the criteria than bulk updates. However, deletes that meet the criteria can often be handled *much* more efficiently by partitioning on the basis of the sets of rows which it is known will all be deleted at the same time. These sets of rows can then be deleted by dropping the partition which contains them. This is the most common strategy used for manual partitioning in Oracle7, and it's the one which we've seen tested using Oracle8 partitioning.

Whatever strategy you pick, be sure that you don't change the partitions in which rows will reside—unless you are prepared to explicitly design the required delete and insert logic. You can update partition keys, but only if the key change doesn't require the row to be moved to another partition. In this connection we need to make certain assumptions: since the objective of partitioning is to distribute the table, you must have partitions of roughly equal size, and you must be very careful to pick a partition structure that you can live with. If you need to change the structure later on, it won't be easy; you will have to scan and reload all of the data in the affected partitions. Oracle provides a set of ALTER TABLE options to do this, but they take a long time to run on large data volumes. In addition, although there is a SPLIT PARTITION option, there is no MERGE PARTITIONS option (or at least not yet—it seems like an obvious candidate for implementation in the future).

TIP	Oracle allows you to create partitions without specifying names for them, just as it allows you to create unnamed constraints. As with constraints, the server will manufacture a name for any unnamed partition, and you will have to re- trieve this name from the data dictionary if any future oper- ation needs to reference this particular partition—for example, to DROP or SPLIT it.
	We strongly recommend that at your site, you require that all partitions be explicitly named. We recommend that you use the same convention we've used in this chapter—using the partition range in its name. However, there is no need to pre- fix the partition name with the table name; after all, the *namespace* for partition names is the object, rather than the schema.

The purpose of a partitioning strategy is to reduce the unit size of failure. For that reason, most strategies involve at least double-digit numbers of partitions; we've even seen a table with more than 1,000 partitions (each partition covering a single day of a three-year period). If we want to come up with a different strategy for our CALLS table, we could simply inspect each column as a candidate for the partition key (and, if single columns are not selective enough, we can inspect combinations of columns). In fact, in our CALLS table we might have to decompose the call_from column in order to partition on the area code or exchange code. However, in North America if we tried to partition on the three-digit area code this would introduce massive skew into the distribution. Why? Because many more calls are made in the New York area code 212 than are made in the Alaska area code 907. If New York (Los Angeles or Chicago, for that matter) is going to determine the size of our unit of failure, then we'll probably conclude that having a few dozen much smaller partitions is not really very helpful; therefore, we'll try to put a number of them in the same partition. Unfortunately, doing so is made much more complex by the syntax used to specify partition key range values (all of the keys in a given partition must be in a continuous range).

A general rule of design is that every table should have a primary key, and the larger the table, the more mayhem is likely to result if we relax this restriction. Clearly, at least the largest tables—the partitioned tables— must have primary keys. But giving these tables primary keys will have the result of depriving us of partition independence—we must have the table's primary key index available in order to enforce uniqueness at the table level. What can we do? We can *equi-partition* the table and the unique index. If we do this, then as long as the required index partition is available, we'll be able to insert into the table partition and enforce the constraint. Equi-partitioning is illustrated in Figure 4-2 and is discussed in greater detail in the section called "Partitioned Indexes."

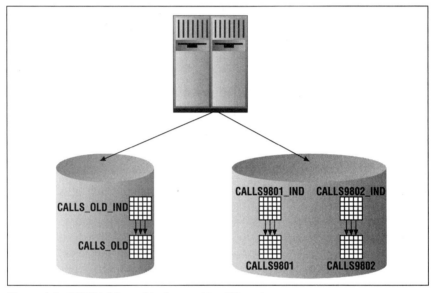

Figure 4-2: CALLS table and index equi-partitioned

Most tables have relationships with other tables. Although many data warehouse applications only need to partition a single fact table, some transaction processing applications may benefit from partitioning both the master and the child tables in a master/detail relationship. To promote partition independence, it may be desirable to equi-partition these two tables. If we do this, a logical problem arises: normally, detail tables are substantially larger than master tables, so for operational reasons, it may be convenient to have more detail table partitions than master table partitions.

If the master table partition key is part of the detail table partition key, then we can maintain a strong measure of partition independence. It's now possible to define a restricted set of partitions which are required for full master/detail operation with any given master, as shown in Figure 4-3.

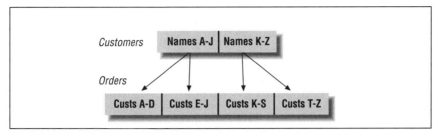

Figure 4-3: A set of partitions for master/detail operation

Date-based partitioning

As we have seen in the examples so far, the partition key is usually either a date or a period code, such as a week number or a month number. (The difference between the two is important; we discuss it in a later section, called "Determining the partition key.") Oracle8 provides a number of DDL (Data Definition Language) operations against partitions, With these statements, we can quickly drop partitions from a table, or add them to a table (although when adding a new partition, loading the data may take a significant amount of time). In our telephone example, when the time comes to drop all the "calls" data for periods before January 1998 and enter the calls data for March 1998, we can accomplish both operations with this simple DDL script:

```
ALTER TABLE calls DROP PARTITION calls_old;
ALTER TABLE calls ADD  PARTITION calls9803
    VALUES LESS THAN ('01-APR-98') TABLESPACE ts98;
```

Of course, in the modified table we can still enter calls for 1997 (or, indeed for 1947) because the partition keycalls_date has no start date; it has only an end date which is the day before the value supplied in the DDL. The program issuing the statement receives an Oracle error if you attempt to insert a row whose partition key is too high; in our calls table, this would start to happen if the DBA were late adding the new partition, or if one of the exchanges has been running with its date incorrectly set.

Oracle8 allows you to specify the keyword MAXVALUE in place of a literal value for the high value of a column of the partition key; for example:

```
ALTER TABLE calls ADD  PARTITION calls9804
    VALUES LESS THAN (MAXVALUE) TABLESPACE ts98;
```

You might decide to use MAXVALUE as the limit value for the partition with the highest partition key range to avoid excluding any partition key values. Even NULLs are allowed because when a partition exists whose high value is MAXVALUE, then partition keys with NULL values will be directed to that partition.

TIP   We advise you not to use MAXVALUE for the upper range of date-based partitioning when you know that another partition will have to be added later on. Why? Because in order to add a new partition, you'll have to split the existing high partition. On the principle that partitioning is used only where there are high data volumes, you must expect that the partition splitting will consume a lot of resources.

MAXVALUE may be acceptable in cases where the highest partition is expected to receive only a handful of rows and will be replaced by a fully bounded partition before it starts to grow to any appreciable size.

In data warehouse and EIS applications, date-based partitioning makes it easy for the DBA to efficiently remove older data once it is no longer required online. We expect this feature to be used extensively for this reason.

Using partitions explicitly

Oracle8 does not force the user of a partitioned table to use partition transparency. You can specify both query statements (SELECT) and DML statements (INSERT, DELETE, UPDATE, and LOCK) against a specific named partition; for example:

```
SELECT call_from
     , call_start
     , call_seconds
  FROM calls PARTITION (calls9804)
 WHERE call_to = 8006722538;
```

This query has the effect of using the partition key range as an "index"; it will return only from the subset of calls (those calls made in April 1998). Strangely, even though the syntax requires you to specify the partition name within parentheses, it does not allow you to retrieve from multiple partitions. So if you want all the calls for both February and April you must either:

- Return to partition transparency and write the query with a WHERE clause, exactly as you would for a table which was not partitioned, or

- Write the query as a UNION ALL for a query against CALLS9802 and another against CALLS9804 (this is starting to become rather arcane).

Neither PL/SQL nor distributed SQL support explicit partition referencing. With PL/SQL, a workaround is to use dynamic SQL within the PL/SQL. With distributed SQL, you can perform retrieval in a remote stored procedure that uses dynamic SQL. (We doubt that you'll encounter many cases where you'll decide that explicit partition referencing is worth the bother of these workarounds.)

In one specific case, we consider explicit partition referencing to be a truly useful design technique (nevertheless, Oracle8 is still new, and we're not sure how often this case will actually occur in practice). Where a table has been partitioned according to a series of business functions, it seems to make complete sense for each of the functions to explicitly reference its own partition. An example might be a stock movements table which has partitions for internal movements, receiving movements, and shipment movements. Processes which look at movements as a whole would use the table name unqualified by a partition name; however, an application written to handle only internal movements would specify both the table name and the name of the internal movements partition. Of course, this case is somewhat artificial, and it only manages to divide the table into three partitions; some real-world projects that are planning to use table partitioning will be dividing tables into dozens, and in some cases hundreds, of partitions.

NOTE   Specifying the partition name on an INSERT statement has no effect other than to provide an additional level of checking. There are no circumstances under which Oracle8 will store the row in any partition other than the correct one for the value of the partition key.

Specifying the partition name may also be a helpful sanity check when you're writing ad hoc SQL to perform emergency repairs on a section of a partitioned table. In general, we see little reason to specify the partition key in embedded SQL except in heavily engineered projects (where the data dictionary can be looked up at run time by code which then dynamically generates a reference to the correct partition—and there, only in cases where only one partition needs to be accessed). Of course for SELECT, UPDATE, and DELETE operations, Oracle's query optimizer should be capable of doing exactly the same thing—whereas in the beta software which we have been running, it has only been doing so in specific cases. The workaround for this problem is discussed in the next section.

Determining the partition key

In an ideal world, your partition strategy would determine the partition key in a simple way, but in the world of computing, things are not always that simple. Looking again at the U.S. telephone area codes, you can see that it would be impossible to put Alaska (907) in the same partition as Nevada (702) unless that partition also contained Houston (713). This might be exactly what we had planned, but since Houston is the fourth largest city in the U.S., we might actually want it to have a partition of its own. How can we make this work? We can add another field to the row (as if the table is not large enough already!) and use a translation table to map our logical partition key to a physical partition key. Here is the example:

Area_Code	Partition_Key
212	1
...	
702	30
...	
713	4
...	
907	30

The additional space and CPU load involved in performing the mapping and handling of the additional table column aren't so severe that we're likely to abandon partitioning entirely, but they do represent an unwanted overhead, and add complexity to the application. This book is about Oracle8, not about general design principles, but we do feel obliged to make a general comment: each additional complexity in a data structure makes it more likely that the people who write code to handle the structure are going to make mistakes. Oracle has triggers that should allow you to hide the additional column on the INSERT, unfortunately, triggers don't fire during high-speed loading. Catch-22 again!

How about the solution of equi-partitioning the table and the primary key index? Unfortunately, we can't use this feature because the partition key has no place in the primary key. If we want to partition the primary key index in this case, the best option is to use the area code as the partition key and to simply put up with the inconvenience resulting from the distribution of area codes. Although we can have multiple, numerically adjacent smaller area codes in the same partition, we don't have the degree of freedom we might like to have.

Let's go back to using the calendar as our partition strategy. We're more comfortable with this approach anyway, because we already know that we need to be able to remove one month at a time from the table; we also know that we can do this very efficiently using one partition per month. In addition, although there may be seasonal peaks in the total number of calls, each partition will be approximately the same size. Also, the partition key is part of the primary key, so we will not need a global unique index to maintain primary key integrity. Great all around!

When we issue a query such as the following:

```
SELECT  call_from, call_to, call_start, call_seconds
  FROM  calls
 WHERE  call_secs >  86400 /* calls longer than 24 hours */
   AND  call_start BETWEEN '03-MAR-98' and '10-MAR-98';
```

it will only need to scan the March 98 partition. Well, it only needs to scan that one partition, but our tests indicate that it actually scans all of them. However, if we change the query to contain an equality on the partition key (in this case, only reporting for a single day)

```
SELECT  call_from, call_to, call_start, call_seconds
  FROM  calls
 WHERE  call_secs >  86400 /* calls longer than 24 hours */
   AND  call_start = '03-MAR-98';
```

then the optimizer spots that all of the qualifying rows must lie within the March 98 partition and scans only that partition.

We've managed to work around this problem by creating partitioned indexes (as we describe in the next section), but we've found that the EXPLAIN PLAN output for such queries appeared to be misleading. In the end, we tested which partitions were being accessed by placing the various partitions in different tablespaces and putting offline the tablespaces that didn't logically require access. Then, if the query ran without error, we knew that it hadn't tried to access any partitions other than those that we expected it to access.

We ran these tests against an early version of Oracle8 and in the time we had available, we weren't able to find an effective workaround. (Let us know what you come up with!) Our advice: before you rely on any specific performance claims, test carefully the extent to which the query optimizer is using knowledge of your partitioning structure.

Of course, there are ways of getting this to work. Adding an explicit partition reference will solve the problem as in this example:

```
SELECT  call_from, call_to, call_start, call_seconds
  FROM  calls PARTITION (calls9803)
```

```
WHERE  call_secs >  86400 /* CALLS LONGER THAN 24 HOURS */
  AND  call_start BETWEEN '03-MAR-98' and '10-MAR-98';
```

We wouldn't recommend this as a solution. A truly robust implementation requires the use of a query generator. That generator interrogates the Oracle data dictionary and performs the analysis that we believe ought to be performed in the data dictionary (to avoid hard-coding too much "knowledge" into our queries). We're hoping for a future solution in which the query optimizer recognizes predicate key ranges which are entirely within a single partition or a subset of partitions.

Partitioned Indexes

Just as Oracle8 allows you to split an unclustered table into a number of partitions (each of which can have its own storage parameters), it also allows you to split indexes into partitions. As with table partitions, index partitions can have their own storage parameters, and the individual partitions can be in different tablespaces.

Partitioned indexes have two forms: *local* and *global*. A locally partitioned index has one dedicated index partition per table partition, whereas a globally partitioned index has a partition structure that's independent of the way in which the table is partitioned. Note that local prefixing is not supported for bitmapped indexes.[*]

Locally partitioned indexes are *prefixed* if the table partition key is at the leading edge of the index; globally partitioned indexes cannot be prefixed in Oracle8, but this is not a severe restriction—it's hard to imagine a reason for wanting to prefix a globally partitioned index.

TIP   You can't build an index on a partition—indexes must be built on either a table or a cluster. But with local prefixed indexes, you can essentially create an independent index for each partition of a table. As long as the table partition and index partition are both usable, you will be able to make any legal indexed use of table partitioning.

Each of the three possible forms of partitioned indexes (global, local, and partitioned) has specific uses, which we discuss later in this section. Oracle8 places no restrictions on the use of nonpartitioned indexes with partitioned tables, or on the use of partitioned indexes with nonpartitioned tables. But we can't think of many cases where an index is likely

---

[*] Some of the early Oracle8 documentation states that partitioned bitmapped indexes are not supported.

to merit partitioning when the table on which it's based is not partitioned. On the other hand, we can easily envision cases where an index is so much smaller than the table on which it is based that, although the table merits partitioning, the index does not.

Some of these concepts are depicted in Figure 4-4.

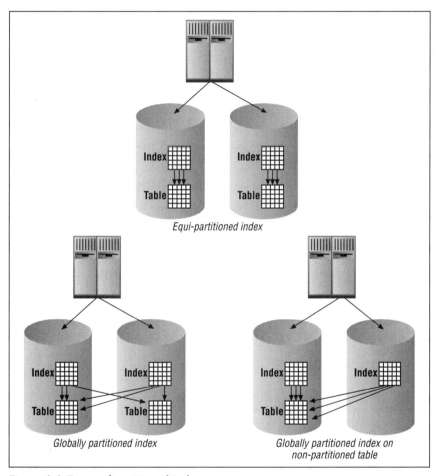

Figure 4-4: Forms of partitioned indexes

Each form of index partitioning can exhibit partition independence. With any index against a partitioned table, there is also partition independence at the table level. This way, an index lookup works if the required index partition is available and is usable, and an index lookup is capable of causing a row fetch if the required table partition is also available. For this reason, locally partitioned indexes (where the index and table are equi-partitioned) exhibit the best availability characteristics.

Unusable index partitions

Unique indexes support both queries and constraint enforcement. If the index (or at least the required partition) is not available, the constraint can't be enforced, and therefore DML against the data can't be permitted. For this reason, wherever possible, make unique indexes locally, rather than globally, partitioned.

In Oracle, nonunique indexes are used solely to support query processing (including the query phase of update and delete operations).[*] Note that it is safe to update the table (or partition) even if the index is not available. However, if you do update the table, the index will now be out of date. In this case, it will be marked as being unusable until it has been rebuilt, which may take time.

Locally prefixed partitions

In situations where we need an index whose leading edge is also our table partition key, we get the tightest integration and the most obvious integration between table partitions and index partitions. Whenever an index lookup is required, the optimizer can tell from the data dictionary in which index partition the key will reside (if it exists). Only that index partition needs to be available for the lookup to be carried out. Because the index partition is local, if DML takes place against a table partition, then only one index partition must be available for you to guarantee that the index will be kept up to date. At first glance, this situation may appear to be the preferred form for partitioning an index, but there are a number of other considerations; we don't support basing the selection of a partition key for a table on the designer's desire to use a locally prefixed partitioned index.

Locally non-prefixed partitions

Unfortunately, it may be difficult to find a concatenated key which is genuinely useful and which has the partition key at its leading edge. In our telephone calls example, it's likely that most predicates on call_start_ time will be in the form of a range (BETWEEN operator). We could decompose call_from into a region or area code and the number within the region. If we made that column the leading edge of the primary key, we'd expect to see at least some queries specifying equality on it. In this

---

[*] There is a notable exception to this rule. Oracle uses foreign key indexes at the child end of a foreign key constraint; it does this to avoid the need for a table-level share lock when updates are taking place against the parent end of the relationship. This exception doesn't invalidate the point we're discussing; the update can still take place even if the index is not available.

case, it might be useful to place the call_start as the next column in the key in order to scan the index efficiently for queries of the form:

```
SELECT  COUNT(*)
  FROM  calls
 WHERE  from_area = 512
   AND  call_start BETWEEN '14-FEB-98' and '15-FEB-98';
```

Because the table partition key is still part of the primary key, the advantage of local partitions during DML is maintained. It's still possible for lookups to be analyzed in enough depth to restrict them to a single partition (or, if the range spans multiple partitions, to a set of partitions). As we said earlier, in preproduction releases of Oracle8, this optimization was not performing as well as we would have liked.

TIP   To create a unique index as locally partitioned, the table
             partition key must be part of the index key.

Of course, tables, even "big" tables, can require nonunique indexes that don't contain their partition key. You can create such tables again as locally partitioned, and in this way they retain the advantage that DML against a given table partition will affect only one partition of the index. However, every lookup will have to visit every partition of the index. Whether this represents a performance problem in your own application depends on a number of factors:

- How often these lookups occur

- How many partitions there are

- How many of the index branch blocks are cached

In a data warehouse or decision support environment where thousands or millions of rows satisfy the query predicates, the additional index block visits may be insignificant. On the other hand, in a transaction processing environment where at most two or three rows will satisfy the query, then the additional block visits may double or triple the statement processing time.

Global partitions

If we have a situation where we need to enforce the uniqueness of a key that doesn't contain the table partition key, we must use either a nonpartitioned index or a globally partitioned index. The choice between the two depends, as usual, on manageability. An update on any table partition may require any index partition, but we can still operate without specific index partitions as long as no new keys are derived that belong in their partition. Thus, if the pattern of key generation has a predictable distribution, we might get some significant administrative and availability benefits from partitioning the index. However, if the index isn't especially large and if new keys arrive more or less randomly throughout the key range, then there seems to be little point in partitioning it at all.

Here's another example of a benefit from a globally partitioned index. Consider a mailing list where the table is partitioned on the basis of the zip or postal code. We need to use this table to look up customers by name alone. With even a few hundred million names and addresses in our mailing list, it may still be a marginal call as to whether the name index really needs to be partitioned. Nevertheless, there is a clear performance advantage in global partitioning because by accessing a single partition, we can guarantee to find all of the hits against a single name.

```
CREATE INDEX mlist_names ON mlist (last_name, first_name)
GLOBAL PARTITION BY RANGE
( PARTITION ad VALUES LESS THAN ('E')
, PARTITION eg VALUES LESS THAN ('H')
, PARTITION hm VALUES LESS THAN ('N')
, PARTITION nt VALUES LESS THAN ('U')
, PARTITION uz VALUES LESS THAN (MAXVALUE)
);
```

The performance boost we'll get in transaction processing from having only one index tree to navigate may outweigh the availability considerations.

As usual, you'll need to make design decisions regarding partitioned tables by comparing the strengths and weaknesses of the possible solutions.

Index-Only Tables

Sometimes, the primary key of a table comprises most of the columns in the table, and in many cases the primary key is the entire row. Typical examples are:

- Single-column lookup tables where the code is self-explanatory and requires no description—for example, state or currency

- Intersection tables used to resolve many-to-many relationships where the relationship has no attributes of its own—for example, a languages_spoken table which might be an intersection between employees and languages; we assume here that you don't need to know the person's level of proficiency in the language.

In Oracle7 and Oracle6, the same information that is held in the index (given that the leaf blocks aren't compressed) is repeated in the data blocks. In many cases, each record is held three times: once in the table, once in an index on (language_code, emp#), and once in an index on (emp#, language_code).

If we make the skill level a separate entity with a skill_code, we can represent our languages_spoken table as a three-way intersection and build even more indexes on it. Since every query which uses these indexes can be (and is) completely resolved without reference to the table, the table itself is a "waste of space" (like the universe in the movie *Contact* or the Spanish waiter Manuel in the television show "Fawlty Towers"). However, unlike Manuel, it also has to be both backed up and restored.

Oracle8 sets out to overcome such problems with a new type of object called an index-only table. In fact, many people might consider it to be an index without a table, or even an index-only index. Syntactically, the object is manipulated as a table, so we'll just have to let Oracle have its way and call it an index-only table. A number of designers and DBAs have been getting quite excited about this feature, but we advise you to use caution: there are a number of restrictions which you need to consider before you decide to use index-only tables to save space (as well as backup and recovery time).

The first disappointment arises if we take a conventional structure such as the following:

```
CREATE TABLE part_usage
    ( used_by_part#  NUMBER(8,0) NOT NULL
    , used_in_part#  NUMBER(8,0) NOT NULL
    , quantity_used  NUMBER(8,0) NOT NULL
    , PRIMARY KEY (used_by_part#, used_in_part#)
    );
```

When we insert a row into the table, about 75% of the CPU which is used is expended on the index maintenance. So not having the table at all will save us about 25% of the insert time for each row, one block visit per query (with perhaps another 25% saving in CPU time), and some disk space—potentially useful savings, but not a massive incentive.

The situation is worse if we have to load a large number of these records. In a conventional table, we would disable the primary key constraint, use the high-speed loader, and then re-enable the constraint. This is an order of magnitude faster than loading with the index enabled (and remember that neither SQL*Loader direct path nor INSERT

APPEND is supported on tables of ORGANIZATION INDEX). To create the index-only equivalent of the part_usage table, we need only issue:

```
CREATE TABLE part_usage
    ( used_by_part#  NUMBER(8,0) NOT NULL
    , used_in_part#  NUMBER(8,0) NOT NULL
    , quantity_used  NUMBER(8,0) NOT NULL
    , PRIMARY KEY (used_by_part#, used_in_part#)
    )
    ORGANIZATION INDEX;
```

There are several restrictions:

- The row length must not exceed 50 bytes, although an extension to the syntax allows you to overcome this restriction using an overflow segment. Of course, as soon as you do this, the major performance advantage of the index-only table is lost because to retrieve the data you must now navigate from the index leaf block to where the rest of the row is held. But at least the key data is stored only once.

- You cannot load the table using CREATE TABLE...AS SELECT..., but you can insert into the table using a subquery, so this is not a major restriction.

- You cannot partition the table; this is a pity since the technique seems most appropriate for very large intersection tables.

Of course in the real world, many tables that are called intersection tables have columns which are not part of the primary key. The part_usage table shown in the previous example has a non-key column, quantity_used, showing how many of one part are used inside another part. Clearly, the higher the percentage of the row which is non-key data, the lower the percentage of savings from using an index-only table, and the greater the liklihood of having to use overflow segment space. As we saw above, use of an overflow segment removes the principal performance advantage of index-only tables.

Traditionally, many intersection tables have two unique indexes containing the same two foreign keys but in a different order. However, if we had a normal intersection table, languages_spoken, between employees and languages, we could use an index on (emp#, language_code) to find all of the languages spoken by a given employee. We could use another index on (language_code, emp#) to find all of the employees who speak a given language. And we would not have to visit the table at all.

Now you encounter the really bad news. You cannot currently build an index against a table of organization index. As a result, if in our example you also need an index on (used_in_part#, used_by_part#) and you are determined to use index-only tables, then you only have two solutions (that we've been able to find):

1. Your application has to be coded to maintain both indexes (sorry, we meant tables). This breaks one of the golden rules of indexation, which is that the application code should not need to know how it is done.

2. The second index-only table must be maintained by a trigger on the first. Triggers are supported, and using this workaround at least encapsulates the problem in the definition of the index-only table.

Interestingly when we tried to create an index on the part_usage table, we got the following error:

```
SQL> CREATE INDEX part_usage_reverse ON part_usage
     (used_in_part#, used_by_part#);
                                         *

ERROR at line 1:
ORA-25182: feature not available yet
```

We would like to conclude from this message that indexes on index-only tables will arrive soon. At that point, you can drop the triggers that you will need today to maintain indexes on index-only tables and do the entire job declaratively—that is how it should be.

WARNING   We expect that a number of designers will want to use tables of ORGANIZATION INDEX because they begrudge holding the same data twice with no apparent useful benefit. We see the attractions of the feature, but the space saving is likely to be significant only for very large tables. In this case, the overhead of having to maintain the index during load may render the technique unusable.

Reversed Key Indexes

At first glance, reversed key indexes are bizarre—why on earth would anyone want to hold an index key backwards? Young children sometimes write words backwards as a simple form of cryptography, but that is not the purpose of the feature. It exists simply as a highly effective workaround for a known performance problem with ascending index keys.

If every new key which is added to an index is higher than the previous highest key (often one higher if it is based on an Oracle sequence), then with many users performing insertions in parallel, the users have to contend for the end block of the index leaf set. A common workaround in the past has been to take the next available key and transform it in some way, such as moving the rightmost digit to the leftmost position. This meant that there would be ten, rather than one, index leaf blocks to which new keys would be directed. Reversed key indexes provide the workaround within the schema definition so you don't need to code it within the application.

Use these indexes only when you need the workaround because (for reasons which we hope are obvious to you) reversed key indexes can only support lookup on equality; they do not support range scans.

Those of you who have read *Oracle Design* will also be aware that we are not great advocates of surrogate keys—but we are realists. We know that there are a lot of applications out there in the real world that allocate keys from a sequence or a similar mechanism and which use these keys only for equi-joins. If these applications are suffering from index leaf block contention during multi-user insert operations, then the reversed key index can deliver a highly effective performance boost.

Another potential benefit is that because insertion into a reversed key index prevents new entries from always being made at the end of the sequence set (the index leaf blocks), it is possible for such inserts to take advantage of distributed free space within the index and to reuse space which had been occupied by deleted keys. With a conventional B*tree index, we always advise setting PCTFREE to 0 if all new keys are to be added at the end of the key range. However, with a reversed key index which is known to be subject to a 25% growth, recreating or rebuilding the index with PCTFREE set to 20 should be sufficient to allow all of the new entries to be inserted without any need for space management. (The PCTFREE figure of 20 rather than 25 is correct—think of each index block as having five equal parts of which four are in use after the index build, and one is available for the 25% growth.)

Unstructured Data and LOBs

This section describes Oracle8's support for new datatypes intended for use with long and unstructured data. It looks at the new features (the LOB and BFILE datatypes and the DBMS_LOB package) and at the design considerations for these features.

Actually, despite their name, LOBs (large objects) are not part of the Oracle8 object support. The LOB functionality is included with Oracle8 whether or not the objects option is present. This feature is aimed at improving the server's ability to handle long, opaque, scalar values. It allows a value to be up to 4 gigabytes long, and also stores the value in a separate segment from the rest of the row. From within PL/SQL and OCI, a LOB value can be read and written in chunks. In many ways, the calls available from PL/SQL and C/C++ are analogous to those provided by operating systems to handle serial files. Indeed, one of the supported forms of LOB storage is an operating system file.

The DBMS_LOB package is created when Oracle8 is installed, and it allows a character LOB to be tested to see whether it contains a particular string. In other words, by using PL/SQL functions, it is now possible to operate on "long" values of up to 4 gigabytes from within a conventional SQL statement.

Long and Unstructured Data in Oracle7

Storing unstructured data in an Oracle database has long been the bugaboo of Oracle designers. Yes, Oracle has supported long datatypes (LONG and LONG RAW) for several releases and has enhanced them a few times, but the following restrictions still apply to these datatypes in Oracle7 today:

- Only one long column is allowed per table.

- Long columns cannot be indexed.

- SQL functions and expressions cannot reference long columns.

- Full table scans on tables containing long columns are slow because Oracle has to scan past the data contained in the long column.

- Tables containing long columns cannot be replicated or participate in two-phase commit (2PC).

- Tables with long columns cannot be used as the source of a CREATE TABLE ... AS SELECT statement.

- Long columns cannot be referenced in INSERT INTO ... SELECT FROM statements.

- Constraints cannot be defined on long columns, or be referenced in constraints.

- Long columns cannot be used to order or group queries.

- Snapshots cannot contain long columns.

- Whenever any reference is made to part of a row, the entire row has to be assembled within Oracle's buffer pool. This includes the entire long column—even if it is not required.

The *ConText* option of the Oracle server was helpful in addressing at least one of these issues. ConText makes searches on long columns possible. This still leaves a lot of restrictions on LONG and LONG RAW, even in Oracle8. Rather than trying to fix the deficiencies in the current long datatypes (which would have meant making changes that impacted existing code), Oracle has chosen to implement a whole new family of datatypes, known as LOBs.

Introducing LOBs

Oracle8 supports a new object type, known as a *large object* or *LOB*, which is designed to store unstructured data. There are four basic LOB datatypes:

BFILE
> A LOB whose content is not stored in the database but is held in an external data file

BLOB
> A LOB containing raw or binary data

CLOB
> A LOB containing single-byte character data

NCLOB
> A LOB containing multi-byte character data (e.g., national character sets); note that NCLOBs cannot contain varying-width national character sets

Each occurrence of a LOB may contain up to 4 gigabytes of data. LOB data can be manipulated in two different ways:

- Through a PL/SQL package called DBMS_LOB
- Through a series of API calls from the Oracle Call Interface (OCI).

PL/SQL8 also provides a set of intrinsic datatypes for the support of LOBs; although SQL cannot directly manipulate these datatypes, they are accessible from SQL through PL/SQL function calls.

Figure 4-5 illustrates the difference between a BFILE and the other various LOB datatypes.

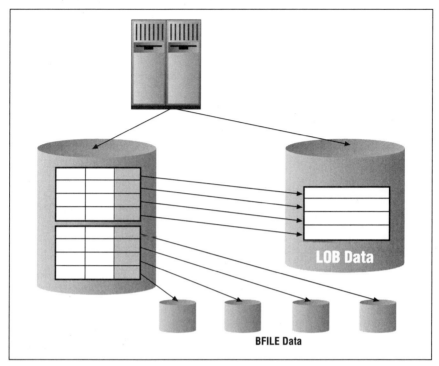

Figure 4-5: The difference between BFILEs and the other LOBs

The functions and procedures available through the DBMS_LOB package are summarized in Table 4-1.

Table 4-1: DBMS_LOB Package Functions and Procedures

Name	Purpose
APPEND	Appends the contents of one LOB to another.
COMPARE	Compares the contents of two LOBs of the same type (or parts of the LOBs).
COPY	Copies the contents of one LOB to another.
FILECLOSE	Closes the file pointed to by the specified locator.
FILECLOSEALL	Closes all BFILEs open in the current session.
FILEEXISTS	Checks whether the file pointed to by a given BFILE locator exists.
FILEGETNAME	Determines the directory and filename of a given BFILE.
FILEISOPEN	Checks whether the specified BFILE is open.
FILEOPEN	Opens a specified BFILE.
ERASE	Erases all or part of the contents of a LOB (not the same as setting a LOB to NULL).
GETLENGTH	Returns the length of the given LOB (in bytes or characters, depending on the LOB type).

Table 4-1: DBMS_LOB Package Functions and Procedures (continued)

Name	Purpose
INSTR	Returns the offset of the nth occurrence of the given pattern in the LOB.
READ	Reads a chunk of an LOB into a supplied buffer.
SUBSTR	Returns a part of a LOB from a given offset and length.
TRIM	Reduces the size of a LOB occurrence by removing characters or bytes from the end.
WRITE	Writes to an area of a LOB from a given offset for a given number of bytes.

LOBs are physically separated from the rest of the structured data in the same row. The row carries a *locator* which is similar to a pointer in a programming language. When a new row is created, the locator is, by default, null. Before the LOB or BFILE data can be populated, you must initialize the locator by calling the EMPTY_BLOB or EMPTY_CLOB function. Once you've set up the locator, you can call the LOB functions listed in the table to populate it and manipulate the data. By separating the LOB data from the rest of the row data, Oracle solves the problem of slow full table scans. (This works because the LOB data doesn't need to be read.)

There is another benefit to this approach. Because the LOB data is in a separate segment, with its own storage parameters and space management strategy (or, in the case of BFILE, is in an external file), the designer is no longer faced with trying to accommodate both short structured records and long unstructured records within a single table. In the past, the only way designers have been able to deal with this situation was to use a compromise strategy that wasn't ideal for either record type.

Design Considerations

There are some decisions you need to make as a designer before you begin to use the new large object features.

BFILE or LOB

When you are designing for long unstructured data, which datatype should you use, LOB or BFILE? The answer, as you have probably guessed, is "it depends." If you need the data to participate in database transactions, use a LOB. If the data doesn't need to participate in database transactions, and if the data is received from an external source as a file, then use a BFILE.

BFILEs are attractive since there is no overhead involved in loading them. But there are several issues you need to be aware of when you use BFILEs:

1. Oracle makes no attempt to control what users of the operating system do with external files. Someone might delete or copy another file over your external file. Doing so potentially violates the referential integrity of the data and is always a risk.

2. When a BFILE is deleted from the database, only the database reference is actually deleted, and the file remains unaffected. When you use BFILEs, you need to design periodic processes that clean up orphan BFILEs whose references have all been deleted or which were created as part of a transaction which rolled back. Of course, with data held inside the database, Oracle has more control over who accesses and updates the data, and manages the housekeeping tasks of cleaning up deleted data (and how they perform these operations).

3. If you are using the multi-threaded server (MTS), a session must be bound to a single server while it has a BFILE open. The server process has the file open and the file handle cannot be freely passed between the sessions.

Our general guideline is to use LOBs, rather than BFILEs, except where there are compelling reasons to use BFILEs. An example of such a reason is that the data already exists in external files running into hundreds of megabytes each, and you have little or no need to update the data or inspect it within PL/SQL.

Recoverability and consistency

By default, LOBs (like any other data in Oracle), are subject to read consistency. Read consistency means that the data visible to a query has a read consistency point, usually the time at which statement execution was initiated. If the data has been changed since the read consistency point, Oracle achieves consistency once again by reconstructing the original state from the rollback segments. You can imagine the impact on the current rollback segment and the redo log of inserting or deleting a 4-gigabyte LOB. As a designer, you need to consider this entire issue of read consistency very carefully. Fortunately, the new LOGGING attribute for LOB storage can be set independently of the same attribute for the structured part of the row. This is extremely convenient for the designer, but it can result in some unexpected behavior.

We discuss the considerations surrounding the Oracle8 logging options later in this chapter in the "NOLOGGING Option" section.

Multiple LOBs

You can define multiple LOBs in a single table. For example, a row could contain (or, more accurately, point to) both a video clip and a GIF image. As the example implies, such a technique is particularly useful when you are designing for the World Wide Web.

Using LOBs in cartridges

LOBs are useful in building Oracle data cartridges. You can organize the data in a LOB any way you want, and provide a set of methods to access and manipulate the data. Oracle Corporation itself has developed extensible data cartridges to support technologies such as imaging and document management.

Primary key indexes

To insert a LOB value, you must insert an empty LOB value and then select back the value of the locator. This is shown in the following code fragments:

```
CREATE TABLE lob1
  ( handle    NUMBER PRIMARY KEY
  , text      CLOB
  )
  LOB (text) STORE AS (STORAGE (INITIAL 500K NEXT 500K));
  ...
  clob_loc    CLOB;
  some_text1  VARCHAR2(30000);
  some_text2  VARCHAR2(30000);
  some_handle INTEGER;
  text_lth1   INTEGER;
  text_lth2   INTEGER;
  ...
  INSERT INTO lob1 (handle, text)
    VALUES (some_handle, empty_clob);

  SELECT text INTO clob_loc
    FROM lob1
   WHERE handle = some_handle;

  text_lth1 := LENGTH(some_text1);
  text_lth2 := LENGTH(some_text2);

  DBMS_LOB.WRITE
      (clob_loc, text_lth1,              1, some_text1);
  DBMS_LOB.WRITE
      (clob_loc, text_lth2, text_lth1 + 1, some_text2);
```

Many designers are used to performing bulk loads with primary key constraints disabled in order to eliminate the index maintenance overhead. However, because of the need to select back the row just inserted, the provision of a primary key index is a performance boost when you are loading LOB values into a table with more than a few hundred rows.

Piecewise operations

The example in the previous section shows the insertion of a character LOB in two pieces. In PL/SQL, this would be essential if the total length of the two strings exceeded the longest VARCHAR which PL/SQL can handle (32,767 bytes). We must caution you, though, that there is a CPU overhead for each piece handled. In general, the fewer pieces that are used for any given LOB value, the more efficient the insert or fetch process will be. Therefore, for values of any significant length in PL/SQL, try to keep piece sizes up towards the 32-kilobyte limit. In OCI, handle values in one piece where possible.

When a LOB must be searched procedurally, however, there is a clear exception to this rule. Piecewise fetching makes a lot of sense if your code must hunt through a LOB looking for a particular value or structure within it and if there is a good chance that it will be able to determine the result without having to search the entire LOB value. In such cases, parts of the LOB which are not required for the processing will never have to be fetched.

Supporting Large Populations of Users

As we mentioned earlier, Oracle Corporation claims that Oracle8 supports ten times as many users as Oracle7. An increased user population is made possible by support of a server-based queuing technology and a messaging facility within the server. Essentially, Oracle supports more users by reducing the per-user memory overhead on the server. Although we don't doubt that Oracle8 will be able to support additional users, we expect the maximum number to approximately double, rather than increasing tenfold.

Connection Sharing

Oracle Corporation has made much of the fact that Oracle8 supports "connection sharing," but as far as we can tell, this term refers to the

---

Lessons from the Mainframe

The computer industry is currently making yet another of its infamous U-turns. The departmental computer is now out of vogue, and the mainframe is enjoying a revival. Of course, we don't call these new-generation computers "mainframes." We call them "superservers." But whatever you call them, they must be capable of supporting large numbers of simultaneous users. This section describes some of the Oracle8 features that help support large user populations.

By the way, do you remember the "dumb terminal"? At least one well-known manufacturer used to sell a dumb terminal which actually contained two microprocessors. The dumb terminal concept is now being repackaged and remarketed as the "thin client." Perhaps we are taking things a little too far here, but the point we are trying to make is that in the current computer marketplace, the server is taking on more of the role that traditionally was performed by the client.

Today's server has to support a large user community, mostly connected across a wide area network (WAN), with users increasingly more likely to be running a Web browser than a custom client application written in Oracle Forms or Visual Basic. Or they may be running a custom client application, but it will be one written in Java at the (thin) client and in a 3GL at the server. This dramatic swing in client-server computing has yet to lead to a radical redesign of the way that user connections are handled. Nevertheless, we believe that such a shift is inevitable and that the solution is (as in so many other areas) to adapt the strongest points from traditional mainframe practices.

---

sharing of Net8[*] connections rather than to the sharing of database connections. This seems to be yet another rebirth from the mainframe days—this time, the rebirth of the network multiplexor. Sharing network connections potentially reduces some memory overhead on the server, as well as limiting the number of virtual circuits that must be maintained. However, it fails to address the basic problem that each connection to Oracle uses a great deal of memory.

---

[*] During the Oracle8 beta program the successor to SQL*Net Version 2 was called simply Net3. We suspect that Oracle traditionalists will continue to refer to it as SQL*Net for some years to come. To be fair, the name change has considerable justification since the services within Net3 handle much more than just the transmission of SQL requests and their results. You may be reassured to discover that Oracle has finally learned something from Microsoft—even if it is only how to number software versions. What was called Net3 in beta is now called Net8 in production.

Oracle has continually asked members of the Oracle8 beta program not to use pre-release versions of the software for performance testing, but we can't help noting that under the last beta version, simply connecting to Oracle8 under Windows NT from SQL*Plus consumed about 2 megabytes of memory. SQL*Plus users with mature sessions (those which had been running for some time) used as much as 10 megabytes. Multiply these numbers (or any numbers even remotely close to them) by the 100,000 simultaneous connected users being supported routinely by the largest mainframe OLTP systems, and the nature of the problem starts to come into sharp focus. Needing a terabyte for the database is one thing, but needing it just for *pagefile.sys* is something else again.

We repeat the thesis we discussed at some length in *Oracle Design*: to support a large number of simultaneously connected users efficiently requires connection sharing—typically through a transaction manager. This, in turn, mandates a three-tier architecture. In a three-tier architecture, the presentation logic is typically in the client, the application logic in a middle tier, and the data logic in the data server. We are concerned that Oracle seems to be obscuring this logic from its users, possibly for commercial reasons, because a three-tier architecture places the overall transaction coordination and the role of user authentication and privilege management in the hands of the transaction manager, and it relegates the database server to simply that, a server.

User Identification

True database connection sharing requires that worker tasks in the transaction manager maintain standing database connections which they assign to the processing of (atomic) requests made on behalf of their clients. Typically, each worker task connects as one of a very limited number of "users" which have wide ranging authority (e.g., ACCOUNTS_QUERY_USER, ACCOUNTS_UPDATE_USER, and so on). There is no requirement for the database server to formally recognize the identity of individual users, even though the database itself may well be the repository used by the transaction manager to record user data.

The distinction is important because we can reasonably expect a Web server to have an unlimited number of users. At the time we're writing this book, the potential number is 50 million and growing fast. However, to our great surprise and consternation, Oracle8 has a fixed limit of only 65,535 user IDs. Given the size of some of the organizations that are starting to deploy major Oracle applications, and given the push within Oracle to introduce customers to the benefits of single sign-on, we believe that this limit could pose a major problem to a number of large users.

TIP	Before using Oracle usernames to distinguish individual users of database services, make sure that the total number of such users is well below the published limit.

Bitmap Indexes

Bitmap indexes are not new in Oracle8. They were part of Oracle7, although they arrived at a late stage of its product life. Because these indexes are still relatively new Oracle features, and because their major application is for indexing very large tables, we discuss them briefly in this section.

Although achieving a robust and efficient implementation of bitmap indexes is a major achievement, they are very simple in concept. For each distinct value of the key, the index holds a bitmap which contains one bit for each row in the table. If the bit is on, the row contains that particular key value; if it is off, the row does not contain that key value. Could anything be simpler?

Let's imagine the possible sets of entries in bitmap indexes on both hair color and eye color in a persons table.

Hair Color	Bitmap
Black	0 0 0 0 0 0 1 0 0 0 0 0 0 1 0 0 0 0 0 0 0 1 0 0 0
Dark Brown	1 1 1 0 0 1 0 0 0 0 1 0 0 0 0 1 0 1 0 0 0 0 0 1 1
Light Brown	0 0 0 1 0 0 0 0 1 0 0 1 0 0 0 0 1 0 0 0 0 0 0 0 0
Grey	0 0 0 0 1 0 0 0 0 0 0 0 1 0 0 0 0 0 0 1 0 0 1 0 0
Blonde	0 0 0 0 0 0 0 1 0 1 0 0 0 0 1 0 0 0 0 0 1 0 0 0 0

Because we have identified only five hair colorings in this small population (25 people), we have only five bitmaps in our index. This is not to say that these are the only possible values—the bitmap for any particular value will not be created until the value is found to occur within the table. Therefore, a new bitmap may have to be built as a result of an INSERT or UPDATE operation. Similarly, a bitmap may become redundant as the result of an UPDATE or DELETE operation against the table.

To keep the example simple, we show the eye color index with only four eye colorings in use.

Eye Color	Bitmap
Black	1 0 0 0 0 0 0 0 1 0 0 0 0 0 0 0 0 0 1 0 0 0 1 0
Brown	0 1 0 0 1 0 0 0 1 0 0 1 1 0 1 0 0 1 0 0 1 0 0 0 1
Blue	0 0 0 1 0 0 0 1 0 0 0 0 0 1 0 0 0 0 0 0 0 0 0 0
Green	0 0 1 0 0 0 1 0 0 0 1 0 0 0 0 1 1 0 1 0 0 1 1 0 0

The syntax to create such indexes is intuitive if you already know how to create B*tree indexes in Oracle:

```
CREATE BITMAP INDEX persons_hair_color ON persons(hair_color);
CREATE BITMAP INDEX persons_eye_color  ON persons(eye_color);
```

Now, if we want to locate all of the blue-eyed blondes in our persons table, we submit the following query to Oracle:

```
SELECT first_name
     , last_name
     , gender
  FROM persons
 WHERE hair_color = 'BLONDE'
   AND eye_color  = 'BLUE';
```

Then, to find the rows which qualify, Oracle only needs to access the two bitmaps and AND them together. For example:

```
        0 0 0 0 0 0 0 1 0 1 0 0 0 0 1 0 0 0 0 0 1 0 0 0 0
AND     0 0 0 1 0 0 0 1 0 0 0 0 0 1 0 0 0 0 0 0 0 0 0 0
        ─────────────────────────────────────────────────
        0 0 0 0 0 0 0 1 0 0 0 0 0 0 0 0 0 0 0 0 0 0 0 0
```

We can quickly see that the eighth row in the table is the only one meeting our characteristics. Depending on the types of queries for which we'll use this table, we might need to add further bitmap indexes on attributes such as gender, age group, favorite type of music, and height range.

For many years, Oracle has performed "index merging" on its B*tree indexes, meaning that equalities against two columns have resulted in looking up the respective key in each index and merging the generated ROWID lists. However, since the introduction of Oracle6, the performance of the mechanism has been disappointing (to put it mildly). Bitmaps give us a faster mechanism, and one that's easier to understand. They also give us a mechanism that can be parallelized if the bitmap indexes are partitioned on something other than their own key.

We recommend that you use bitmap indexes primarily in cases where a series of attributes are available on which to index, such as in the persons table above. Ideally, these attributes will not be particularly selective (i.e., they will not have a high number of distinct values). Suppose you know that there will be many queries which will specify equality against more than one of these attributes, but that all of the various possible combinations of key columns are equally likely to appear. We can't solve the problem using B*tree indexes with concatenated keys because we would need too many of them. By opting for a bitmap index on each of the attributes (columns), we can have the query optimizer decide dynamically which ones to scan in parallel and combine using bitwise logic.

TIP   Bitmap indexes are not limited to being single-column in-
            dexes. If necessary, you can specify each bitmap for a com-
            bination of values from 1 to 16 columns, but we doubt that
            there is any valid reason for getting even close to this limit.

            In Oracle7, bitmap index support is available only if you have
            bought the Parallel Query Option (PQO). We aren't currently
            aware whether this policy applies to Oracle8.

Another real penalty of B*tree indexes is their sheer size (a minimum space usage per indexed row of 13 bytes). Oracle rows which have a null value for the key do not appear in the index, so we can't say that the minimum is always 13 bytes per row. For a typical VARCHAR2(2) code in a table of any large size, the number of kilobytes required for a B*tree index on the code column can be guestimated by simply multiplying the expected number of rows by 14 and dividing by 1,000 (or 1,024). At the theoretical level, the minimum space usage in a bitmap index is 1 bit per key value per row, and bitmap indexes are held compressed so that they typically take less space than you'd expect from a raw space calculation. It is not a trivial matter to derive the ROWID (relative block in table, relative row in block) from a bitmap, and therefore there is an overhead for the mechanism used to support this mapping. Nevertheless, in the tests we've performed, bitmap indexes with a restricted number of key values were much smaller than their equivalent B*trees (less than 10% of the size in some cases). Even when we built a bitmap index on a unique key (a silly thing to do), we found that the resulting index was only about 50% larger than the B*tree index which it replaced—although it was somewhat slower at retrieving the rows.

WARNING   During our testing, we discovered, somewhat to our annoy-
ance, that it was not possible to have both a bitmap and a
B*tree index at the same time on the same column or set
of columns. An attempt to create the second index produc-
es the error message:

`ORA-1408: such column list already indexed.`

This is unfortunate; we can conceive of circumstances where
it would be useful to have both a bitmap index (to perform
combined tests on equality across a series of columns) and a
B*tree index (to locate specific key values or ranges of key
values). It is possible to have a redundant column in the table
and to use triggers to ensure that it contains the same value as
the column which you want to carry two indexes. However,
queries must cite the column name which carries the appropriate index for their purpose.

Earlier in this section, we sketched a bitmap index as though it were a
table with one row per key value. In many ways, that is exactly what it is,
and that is how row-level locking is applied to a bitmap index. An exclu-
sive lock is applied to the whole bitmap for the given key. Therefore, any
high frequency of index entry operations involving the same key value
will cause lock conflicts to occur. Since bitmap indexes are more appropriate for keys with a low selectivity (and therefore a high number of
bitmap entries per key), lock conflicts are almost inevitable if bitmap
indexes are used on certain tables. These are tables against which insertions or deletions are performed, or tables where rows have their indexed
column values updated in multi-user operation.

Bitmap indexes are a valuable feature, but they are best restricted to
columns which have a relatively low number of distinct values in tables
maintained by single-stream processing (to avoid the potential for lock
conflicts). Bitmap indexes are useless for supporting BETWEEN operations, but they are very powerful for giving rapid access to intersections
of key values against a number of columns. Such indexes are about the
only viable alternative to full table scans in cases where the combination
of columns which will appear in queries is highly variable. However,
with the Parallel Query Option, full table scans may be a more than
adequate solution. We foresee that bitmap indexes will be extensively
used in data warehouse applications on dimension columns of fact tables,
particularly since these tables are rarely updated.

Cooperative Indexing

Cooperative indexing isn't actually an Oracle8 feature at all, but rather a term for a technique referred to in some of the Oracle8 documentation. It's a series of workarounds which you can apply if Oracle8 itself is unable to support the particular index strategy you want to use. The concept is a valid one, but note that the term "cooperative" is used correctly here, meaning "unless each individual application does it correctly, it will not work." This is the same meaning which we have in mind when we refer to cooperative locking. It's a scheme which, whatever its merits, fails to deliver the correct result unless the applications conform.

We'd prefer that you not rely on application coordination to work around problems such as Oracle's inability to hold a column index in uppercase. A good way is to introduce a trigger-maintained column in the table which holds the uppercase value of the attribute to be indexed. In this way, the indexing itself ceases to be cooperative, although (sadly) the use of the index is still cooperative in that the constructor of the query (an end user, a programmer, or a query generator) has to know which column to use. If the Oracle optimizer sees a query such as the following:

```
SELECT first_name, last_name, post_code
  FROM ...
 WHERE last_name = 'STEVENSON';
```

it has no semantics to help it translate that to the form required to use the uppercase index. Instead, issue:

```
SELECT first_name, last_name, post_code
  FROM ...
 WHERE last_name_upper = 'STEVENSON';
```

It is entirely possible that the first form of the query will miss at least some, and possibly all, of the Stevensons if we assume that their last names have been entered in mixed case.

Oracle strongly suggests that cooperative indexing is a major application for index-only tables, but this supposes that the best way of holding the derived columns is in a separate table. We think that derived columns should be in a table of their own only when the relationship between the source row and the derived column values is one-to-many. If we look at a document indexing system, we might find a table such as the following:

```
CREATE TABLE documents
   ( doc_id  NUMBER NOT NULL PRIMARY KEY
   , summary VARCHAR2(2000) NOT NULL
   -- may contain any number of keywords
```

```
, held_by VARCHAR2(20)    NOT NULL FOREIGN KEY
    REFERENCES keepers
,  ...
);
```

To quickly find documents with combinations of keywords in their summary, we are going to need an index on individual keywords. We already know that trying to hold and index a repeating group in an Oracle table is not a sensible proposition (even though Oracle8 has raised the number of columns allowed per table to 1,000). So we recommend a separate table whose entries are, again, maintained by triggers on the documents table. Clearly, the primary key of this second table will be (keyword, doc_id), and this is likely to be the entire row—but this isn't sufficient reason to make this table into an index-only table. As we discussed earlier in this chapter, index-only tables are subject to a number of formal restrictions; they also have severe performance considerations on loading. Despite the additional space required, we strongly recommend that the second table be a conventional table (even if it were only updated in batch and the number of keywords was low,* then a bitmapped index on keyword might be a major performance boost).

NOLOGGING Option

Oracle7 Release 7.3 added UNRECOVERABLE as an option on INSERT, UPDATE, and DELETE statements. With the coming of this great feature, any application programmer or ad hoc user who had DML access to the table (and who could spell the keyword) was now capable of and, by default, authorized to, start issuing unrecoverable operations. This was not good. In addition to the obvious restriction that these operations would not be recoverable, they also left very little trace. As a result, less honest users now had an almost magic capability—they could make changes to data which not even a redo log "sniffer" could detect. That was the bad news about the UNRECOVERABLE option.

There was also some good news about the UNRECOVERABLE option. In the hands of a capable DBA, it was now possible to perform a number of bulk maintenance operations without having to write the redo log. If a DBA was planning to take a physical backup once the maintenance operations were complete, these redo logs could take a considerable amount of time to write and they were not logically required. Further, although

---

* At the time of writing this book, we do not have enough data to define "low" in this context. We suspect that if the index contained 1,000,000 entries but only 1,000 distinct keywords, then 1,000 might qualify as "low" and 100 almost certainly would qualify.

the SQL*Loader direct path option was available for loading at much greater speed than was possible using INSERT statements, the option wasn't callable programmatically, nor could its commit interval be varied during a run in order to commit at logically valid points. (We discuss these issues in greater detail in *Oracle Design.*)

In Oracle8, you can use a different mechanism to prevent inserted data from being written to the redo log. This mechanism is available only when the DBA has set the object into NOLOGGING mode; for example:

```
CREATE TABLE document_keywords
    ( keyword VARCHAR2(20) NOT NULL
    , doc_id  NUMBER       NOT NULL
    ) NOLOGGING;
```

The purpose of this option is to *allow* insertion into the table with redo logging switched off. To make this work, you must also include an APPEND hint in the INSERT statement, as we describe in the next section.

APPEND Hint

SQL*Loader's direct path option adds data above the table's high water mark; this means that it adds the data into blocks which have not previously contained data for that table.[*] Oracle8 adds a new hint, APPEND, which requests that this mode be used to process an insert and causes all new rows to be placed above the current high water mark. If the table also has its NOLOGGING flag set, then the inserted data will not be written to the redo log—although some redo log activity can be seen to take place, and we believe that this activity is recording the fact that the insert has occurred.

As you might expect, there are a series of restrictions on the use of this hint. The most important is that the statement following the INSERT must be either COMMIT or ROLLBACK. The INSERT doesn't need to be the only statement in the transaction, but it must be the last. We have noticed that if these INSERTs are rolled back, then Oracle's standard rule applies to any additional extents allocated during the INSERT. They remain allocated.

The Oracle documentation also warns that the existence of global indexes, triggers, or referential integrity (RI) constraints on a table will

---

[*] This is not altogether accurate. Of course, the blocks could at some earlier point have been holding rows which were deleted as part of a TRUNCATE TABLE... REUSE STORAGE operation. A TRUNCATE TABLE operation lowers the high water mark to the beginning of the table. However, the way we've put it in the text should be good enough for you to understand the principle—and is a lot easier to express.

cause the APPEND hint to be ignored. We take this to refer only to *enabled* triggers and *enabled* RI constraints. Whatever the precise meaning, it is clear that the user is fully responsible for carrying out any collateral action which would normally have been taken by a trigger or a referential integrity constraint. Unless this action is taken *before* the INSERT, it will have to be deferred to a later transaction because an INSERT /*+ APPEND */ must be immediately followed by COMMIT or ROLLBACK. If the operation is conducted against a partitioned table, then any global indexes will be marked as unusable.

Direct-Path Inserts

The term, *direct-path INSERT*, appears in a number of places in our Oracle8 documentation. It is actually an alternative name for the combination of NOLOGGING and the APPEND hint discussed in the previous sections.

We have not conducted any formal performance testing of this feature, but from our limited use, we can confirm that on large inserts it saves both moderate amounts of CPU and massive amounts of redo log space. Note also that segments containing LOBs don't need to have their LOGGING flag set to the same value as their parent table. It becomes possible to have a table whose structured data is logged and whose unstructured data is not logged. This usage often represents an exception to the general rule that you should always perform a backup immediately after using the APPEND hint.

In *Oracle Design*, we raised a number of questions about the common practice of loading into a holding table and then using INSERT... SELECT... to transfer the data into the tables where it should be. Although here we repeat our advice that you should avoid this practice at all costs, we have to admit that if you use the combination of NOLOGGING and the APPEND hint, you can now operate this unsafe technique more quickly and with much less redo log being generated!

5

Objects

If you are currently designing working, efficient, maintainable applications using Oracle7, then we'll do you a favor and tell you that you may not need to read this chapter at all. In it we present the main features of the object support with which Oracle8 has been released, and we make a series of recommendations about using these features. However, we are of two minds about object orientation. On the one hand, we find that it's valuable in the design of application logic (although we doubt that a fully OO language is needed in every case—and even that statement presupposes that there is some degree of consensus on what constitutes a fully OO language!). On the other hand, we feel strongly that when an Oracle application is storing and retrieving its objects, there are good reasons for it to continue to use the normalized decomposed structures which are the hallmark of a good relational schema design.

Introducing ORDBMS

As we've said, Oracle8 is only the first step in Oracle's journey toward true object orientation. At this point, Oracle8 is an "object-relational" system (see the sidebar), not a fully object-oriented system. This section provides an overview of the Oracle8 object concepts and some of the issues they raise.

Object views were originally offered by Oracle as an aid to converting a relational application to OO; they are now emerging as an important mechanism for building two-way bridges between object-oriented applications and relational schemas. We believe that, for the foreseeable future,

A Question of Terminology

In the terminology which Oracle is now asking us to use, Oracle8 is an ORDBMS—an Object-Relational Database Management System. This addition of the O word to the generic name is interesting in terms of Oracle's marketing approach because the company used to tell us that Oracle7 was simply a DBMS and that we should omit the R word. Now not only has the word "relational" returned, but it has the word "object" in front of it! We might as well put in a second O and talk about a database server which is OO or *object-oriented*. That is certainly something that at least a section of the market has been asking for. Perhaps more significantly, it is a feature that the (R)DBMS suppliers have been competing to provide (much as they competed five years ago to provide the two-phase commit (2PC) feature. As with the introduction of 2PC, which has scarcely become a widely used feature, there is little sign that the user community as a whole is about to make a massive shift to OO. Indeed (again, as with 2PC), the main user of the new technology may turn out to be Oracle itself in the software tools they offer alongside the server.

most enterprise applications will continue to be based on purely relational schemas. As a result, these object views may be useful in presenting the data to OO applications.

At the time we're writing this book, it's difficult to claim that there is anything new or revolutionary about today's object orientation or object technology. In fact, the most surprising feature of the evolution of object-oriented methods may well be that they have managed to develop in parallel with relational databases for such a long time. The basic design tenets of the two approaches have a number of fundamental and apparently irreconcilable differences. You'd expect that these differences would have led to a more heated conflict between the two camps than we've seen to date.

Pick Your Analogy Carefully

The principal friction between the object and relational communities has been about the decomposed nature of storage within a normalized relational schema. To an object partisan, decomposing an object such as an Order, into Order, Order Lines, Stock Allocations, Shipment Records, and Payment Records is automatically bad. It's certainly possible to construct an Order structure in C or C++ (or even an Order

Record Division in COBOL) which will contain all the details known about any given order—its lines, its stock allocations, its shipments, and the resulting payments.

In fact, such composite records were the norm in the early days of computing. Many early systems had a very good reason for using composite records of this type; they had no effective indexed access, so it was imperative to be able to read the "object" which was to be processed in a single operation (typically from a serial device such as a card reader, or later from a tape drive). The structure of the early programming languages did not, however, lead to tidy handling of these objects. Most designers were happy to move to decomposition and, in particular, to third normal form (3NF).

A common analogy used by the object camp is this: when you park your car in your garage (if you are lucky enough to have both a car and a garage with enough space left free in which to park it), then you park it as an object so that it is already assembled for a fast start when you next want to use it. You do not disassemble it into pieces, carefully label the pieces, and arrange them on shelves, only to have to reassemble them the next morning. At this point the object partisan will typically grin fanatically at the proposer of decomposition and, say something like "Answer that. You can't."

If you feel (as we do) that 3NF still has a little going for it, and if you would like to continue to decompose your objects for storage even in a world which increasingly supports Java, then you might like to ask the object partisan the following, equally bizarre question: Would you rather have your clothes stored in complete ensembles stitched together (including having the hosiery permanently attached to the footwear), or would you like to store the shoes in one place, the hosiery in another, the neckties in a third place, and so on? The object partisan will look at you as if you are mad, and ask what this has to do with the subject. (The answer, which you should probably avoid giving, is that it has the same relevance to the subject as his example does—basically, very little.)

Arguments For and Against Decomposition

Let's look a little less whimsically at the arguments for and against decomposition. Using our earlier example of orders, we might arrive at a table model something like the one shown in Figure 5-1.

There are several ways in which we can divide this model into objects. If we are producing invoices, then we might want to step through a set of customer objects, checking each for uninvoiced orders. Alternatively, we

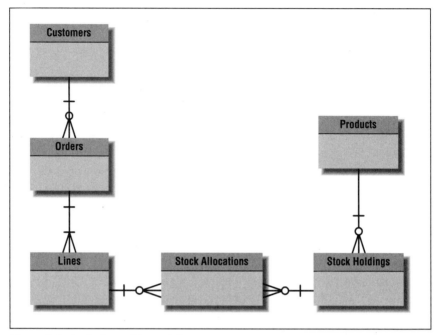

Figure 5-1: An Orders table model

might regard each order (with its lines) as the object and expect this
Order object to contain a link or reference to the Customer object which
describes the person to whom we sold this set of goods (see Figure 5-2).

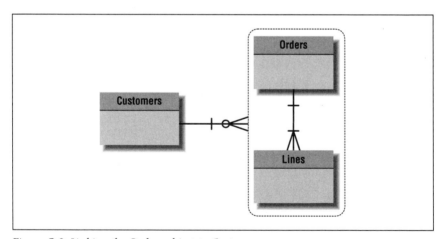

Figure 5-2: Linking the Orders object to Customers

On the other hand, if we need to produce a picking list to issue to store-
keepers so the order can be dispatched, then we would want to add the
Stock Allocations into the Order object (see Figure 5-3).

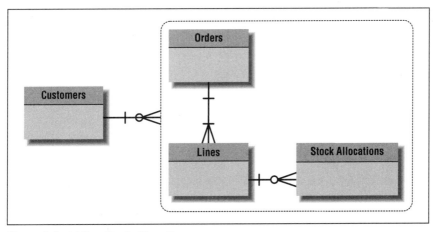

Figure 5-3: Adding Stock Allocations

We now have an object which contains Stock Allocations, which we do not always need when we look at Orders. This is not necessarily a problem as long as fetching the whole object is simple and quick, and as long as we can tell the delivery mechanism that we only want part of the object. However, if we now consider the Stock Holding objects that we might want to process if we are planning to reorder stock, then we start to see a problem (see Figure 5-4).

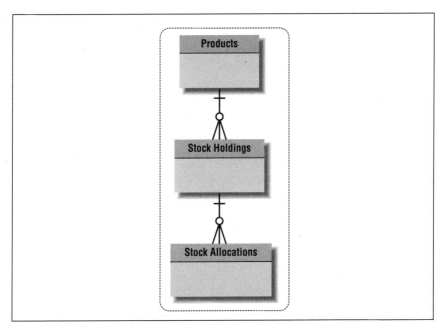

Figure 5-4: Adding Stock Holdings

Stock Allocations are now in two different objects. The solution, of course, is to move Stock Allocations to an object of its own and link this new object (strictly it is not an *object* but an *object class*) to both Orders and Stock. However, this means that our "objects" are increasingly starting to have a one-to-one correspondence with what we previously called tables. Is this actually a problem? In fact, this is exactly how we expect to be able to use the Oracle8 object support successfully in enterprise applications—to allow tables to have a somewhat richer structure than at present.

The Role of the LOB

We don't always need the database schema to have knowledge of the internal structure of an object. In Oracle7, where there was no such need, large objects could be stored using LONG or LONG RAW columns, and in Oracle8, these objects can be handled using LOBs, which are discussed in Chapter 4.

LOBs offer several advantages over LONGs:

- The storage is managed better and the file system can be used to store the data.

- Applications can perform both piecewise fetches and piecewise puts.

- PL/SQL functions can take LOBs (or at least LOB locators) as arguments.

The fact that PL/SQL can process a LOB means that (subject to some efficiency considerations) we can perform tests on LOBs as part of a predicate clause; Oracle8 provides the DBMS_LOB package for this purpose. Chapter 4 describes the use of LOBs and the DBMS_LOB package.

If you want, you can go well beyond this simple usage. Imagine a situation where one of the attributes of a row in a table is an a Microsoft Excel spreadsheet which shows how the Return on Investment (RoI) for a project was derived. The SQL to create this table doesn't need to be complex or contain any profound object syntax:

```
CREATE TABLE projects
    ( proj_id        NUMBER        PRIMARY KEY
    , proj_name      VARCHAR2(30)  NOT NULL
    , manager        NUMBER        NOT NULL
        REFERENCES   project_members
    , roi            BFILE
    -- leave the spreadsheet on the file server
    );
```

At least in theory we can now invent a package—let's call it project_roi—which understands the internal structure of Microsoft Excel spreadsheets and also has knowledge of how the spreadsheets used for a project return on investment are structured. One of the functions in this package might be days_to_break_even. (Since we are talking about objects, perhaps we should refer to it as a method.)

```
CREATE OR REPLACE PACKAGE project_roi AS
   ...
   FUNCTION days_to_break_even(roi BLOB) return INTEGER;
   ...
END;
```

As they say in all the best textbooks, when the author does not have a clue how to do something, "the details of the required function body are left as an exercise for the reader." If we assume that the designer and coder have sufficient skill to solve the problem, then we can imagine a situation in which the following query is fully supported:

```
SELECT p.proj_name
     , roi.days_to_break_even(p.roi)
  FROM projects p
 WHERE roi.days_to_break_even(p.roi) < 360;
```

This approach retains full encapsulation (nothing about the structure of the spreadsheet needs to be known by the person forming the query), but it does raise a number of questions about efficiency and therefore practicality. The only way this query can operate is by performing a full table scan on the projects table and passing each BFILE locator found into the function days_to_break_even. For rows where the predicate is true, the function will be evaluated twice, although this is unlikely to be the major concern.

As we shall see below, there are quite distinct limits on the structures which can be modeled in Oracle8's type system. LOBs give the designer the ability to instruct Oracle to handle complex structures as encapsulated objects, using PL/SQL (or 3GL) code to externalize whatever attributes of those structures are needed to be visible within SQL.

Interfaces

Before introducing the Oracle8 type system, and the facilities it offers designers, we need to give you some warnings about the mechanisms provided for accessing the object features in Oracle8. If you are an experienced Oracle user, then you will know that everything you can do with Oracle can be done through SQL statements and that, without SQL, there is nothing you can do. Over the years, Oracle has developed services such as SQL*Loader's direct path option, which inserts rows into tables without having to use INSERT statements. Such facilities have been the exception, however, and recent releases have offered few of these exceptions. Indeed, Oracle keeps introducing new SQL syntax such as this helpful statement:

```
ALTER SESSION ADVISE ROLLBACK;
```

which puts comments in the DBA_2PC_PENDING views on remote nodes if the session results in the creation of an in-doubt transaction at a remote node. This is admittedly useful, but it's not something that is going to excite the average user or programmer on his first day of a class on relational databases. It's also not in the slightest bit portable to any other DBMS.

Oracle8 object support is different. It provides a number of operations which cannot reasonably be performed using SQL alone. There are also a number of facilities, such as the client-side cache (discussed later), which are handled totally outside SQL with calls which are available only from Oracle's C and C++ libraries. Put another way, if you want to use the whole of Oracle's object support, your choice of implementation language will be between C and C++. No others! Not even the flavor of the month, Java—or at least not yet.

If you are happy to live without the benefits of the client-side cache, then you'll have a few more choices. However, even the object support provided at the SQL level requires syntax which is simply not supported by most of the tools available on the market. It is, however, supported within the latest version of PL/SQL—PL/SQL8. We expect that projects that need to make modest use of Oracle8 object features will be forced to encapsulate most of their object syntax within server-side PL/SQL packages. That's the only way to avoid using SQL syntax which is not supported by their client-side tools.

Are we missing the point? There are already a number of highly successful object-oriented tools which have existed out there in the real world for a good long time without the services of a relational database—and, in some cases, without any formal approach to the problem of persistent storage (as distinct from working storage). It remains to be seen whether the users and vendors of such tools will wish to use Oracle8's type system to model their data structures. Conversely, it also remains to be seen whether these data structures can reasonably be modeled within the Oracle8 type system.

We point out in a number of places in this chapter that you must use either PL/SQL or C/C++ in order to exploit Oracle8's object features.

When working in PL/SQL, the PL/SQL compiler has access to the types defined in the current schema and can derive all of the information which it needs from the online data dictionary.

C and C++ programs do not have the benefit of such a direct interface. For this reason, Oracle has provided a utility called the Oracle Type Translator (OTT) to generate the required structures.

Client-side Cache

A common feature of the objects manipulated by current OO applications is that many of them are large. They may contain a great deal of data, and this data may be of a great number of different types. Let's consider a Project object which might contain the following:

- All versions of the definition of the project deliverables

- All versions of the project plan

- All versions of the project budget

- All staff assignments to and from the project

- All time booked to the project

- All expenditure and income booked to the project

Even if we trim some of these types down from "All versions" to "Current versions", we will still have a great deal of data to hold. Note too that all of this data is structured inside a single object. We might be able to retrieve such objects from the database in a single, fairly efficient operation, but we will then be faced with the problem of how to manipulate this object in program memory. Inevitably, we will find ourselves writing complex code to cope as we add repeating elements in nested structures. As in so many other things, the solution is conceptually simple. We just instruct Oracle's client-side cache to fetch the object (or to initialize an empty one). Then we get things out of it, and put things into it, using the OCI call library for the client-side cache.

Neither of us has written an application which uses the client-side cache and, at the time of writing, neither of us plans to do so in the near future. This is a complex environment that will clearly take some time to learn. However, it does overcome a number of efficiency concerns which exist with the use of some of the features of the Oracle8 object support and, in particular, VARRAYs (variable arrays), which are repeating groups of data stored as part of a row of a table. It is possible to handle VARRAYs entirely within server-side PL/SQL using a series of either packaged procedures or (perhaps more likely) object methods (PL/SQL procedures defined as part of the structure).

If you elect to take this approach, however, you are almost certain to have one of the following problems:

- The number of calls made by the client to the server will rise, and this will cause performance problems. The longer the message round trip time between client and server, the worse these problems will be.

- You will have to find a way to pack the data for transfer between the client and the server so you can make several logical calls at once to your PL/SQL package. While this is completely feasible, it means that you will wind up writing your own client-side cache. Doing so is unlikely to prove a trivial task. In addition, the server-side code will also be, of necessity, complex and therefore error-prone

If you decide while reading the next few pages that the client-side cache is going to help solve some of your design problems, then you may also be committing yourself to using both C/C++ and OCI. If you already are an OCI user and are perfectly comfortable with C/C++, this won't be much of a disincentive. But we know a lot of people who have created major Oracle applications without ever having to learn either OCI or C/C++, and we suspect that they may want to keep it that way.

The Type System

Until Oracle8, Oracle's SQL supported only the scalar primitive types with which it came out of the box. These were modified and added to over the years. The PL/SQL language, as distinct from SQL, brought new types (such as the extremely useful Boolean) and the ability to declare variables of type TABLE and RECORD, specifying the underlying primitive types.

With Oracle8, designers and DBAs can declare their own types within the SQL language and specify that table columns, or whole rows, are of these new types—for example:

```
CREATE OR REPLACE TYPE staff_assignment_o AS OBJECT
    ( staff_id    NUMBER
    , start_on    DATE
    , end_on      DATE
    , recover_at  NUMBER
    ) ;
```

3GLs and Portability

For many years, portability has been one of the reasons why projects battled to avoid 3GLs. Portability is achievable today at the technical level, though it may well remain a political or management hurdle in many organizations. Where decision makers still bear the scars of their doomed attempts over the years to move COBOL applications from one mainframe variant to another, 3GL portability may be assumed not to be feasible.

However, in C and C++ things can be different. If you adhere to POSIX standards, take care with type declarations, and encapsulate all operating system dependencies in functions or through manifest constants, you can ease portability issues. This requires discipline, but it can be done, as Oracle has proven with its highly portable ORDBMS which uses a single set of source code to cover all of the many platforms on which it runs.

Portability itself is irrelevant if every client and every server on the planet uses chips with the same instruction set, operating systems with exactly the same service calls, and database servers with exactly the same interface. But we do not expect that to happen. Or do we?

Reference Pointers (REFs)

Oracle8 supports reference pointers, known as *REFs*, to point from one object to another. The subject of the reference must be an object table, that is, a table which has been defined as being of a particular object type. Therefore, to rework the traditional emp and dept example a little, we could restate the two tables as the following:

```
CREATE TYPE dept_type AS OBJECT
    ( deptno   NUMBER(2)
    , dname    VARCHAR2(14)
    , loc      VARCHAR2(13)
    );

CREATE TABLE dept_t OF dept_type;

CREATE TABLE emp
    ( empno    NUMBER(4)
    , ename    VARCHAR2(10)
    , job      VARCHAR2(9)
    , mgr      NUMBER(4)
    , hiredate DATE
    , sal      NUMBER(7,2)
    , comm     NUMBER(7,2)
    , dept     REF dept_type
    );
```

The syntax allows a REF to be scoped (that is, to be constrained to pointing to a single named table), but scoping is not mandatory. REFs are, however, strongly typed (which is unusual in SQL), and they can only be used to point to an object of the correct type.

Note that the *object table* dept_t requires no new or special syntax to allow full query and DML functionality. To conventional SQL statements, it looks exactly like a conventional table because although each row is an object, the type dept_type uses only built-in types.

Only object tables, that is, tables defined using the syntax CREATE TABLE OF TYPE, can have REFs. Such tables cannot be partitioned, which may limit their use for very large data populations.

REFs have a number of interesting features. An important one is that although there is some enforcement that a REF must be valid when it is stored in a row, there is no enforcement that it remains valid. The result is that the REF user must either provide triggers which prevent the deletion of rows which are the subject of REFs, or all code must regard *dangling REFs* (the case where a REF points at something which no longer exists) to be a normal part of life and handle them appropriately.

TIP   Efficient enforcement by the application of REF integrity
               poses a series of major design problems (which we may
               tackle in some future book); for the moment, we advise us-
               ers of REFs to ensure that their code can handle dangling
               REFs.

We can assign a value to the REF by querying the table to be referenced, for example:

```
UPDATE emp SET dept =
   (SELECT REF(d)
      FROM dept_t d
    WHERE deptno = 10)
 WHERE empno = 7900;
```

Assuming that the REF is still valid at query time, it gives us the ability to perform an "automatic join" in queries such as this one:

```
SELECT dept.dname, ename
  FROM emp
 WHERE job = 'CLERK';
```

This automatic join facility is convenient, and should help to reduce coding errors, but it has a marked potential disadvantage over a traditional foreign key relationship. Even if we only require the value of the foreign key itself, we still have to navigate the REF pointer.

It may be that REFs will give faster navigation from child rows to their parents, but we have rarely (if ever) had performance problems with the use of foreign key links to perform such navigation. As yet, we don't know whether REFs will be appreciably faster than navigating a traditional foreign key relationship, but it is clear that in almost every case they will use appreciably more space. Oracle Corporation has gone to some effort to ensure that such references are globally unique. The VSIZE function reports them as being 36 bytes long. In a detail table with relatively short rows, the use of a couple of REF columns could easily double or triple the overall size of the table.

Abstract Data Types (ADTs)

An abstract data type (ADT) is simply any datatype which is not directly known to the database engine but which can be described through the data dictionary. The first important restriction is that these types must, in the final analysis, map down onto those scalar primitives which come out of the box.

WARNING   Another important restriction is that Boolean is still not available as one of those primitives. On the subject of Booleans, we managed to get the following unattributable quote from one of the (many) Oracle developers at the European Oracle Users' Group meeting in Vienna, April 1997. "We got all the code written but it hadn't passed all the quality gates when we came to the freeze date."

Before we get into the business of *collections* or repeating groups, you need to understand some other features of ADTs in general. Let's assume that the two dates in the staff assignment object are required to be truncated because we have a data rule that part days are not supported by our assignment system. In order to encapsulate the required checking we create a new type, and our example becomes:

```
CREATE OR REPLACE TYPE dateonly           AS OBJECT
    ( value       DATE
    );

CREATE OR REPLACE TYPE staff_assignment_o AS OBJECT
    ( staff_id    NUMBER
    , start_on    DATEONLY
    , end_on      DATEONLY
    , recover_at  NUMBER
    );
```

Sadly, there is no current way to impose declarative constraints on columns in such objects, so although we have the ability to create new datatype names, we cannot easily enforce restrictions on the values that such datatypes can take. This is an important restriction since one of Oracle's major projected uses of an extensible type system was to permit (at last) the implementation of *domains* with the Oracle data dictionary.

A domain is simply a refined datatype: thus we might have a domain called staff_id, a positive nonzero integer which is present as a primary key in the table project_members. We can certainly find a way to create such an object type, but as yet we cannot apply the constraints, making the use of an object type with only one column an unattractive (or certainly unprofitable) proposition.

Each time we create an object type, its members must have names, so dateonly is not just a simple synonym for DATE. If we define a simple example table, the syntax will become clearer:

```
CREATE TABLE events
    ( proj_id    NUMBER      NOT NULL REFERENCES projects
    , event_seq NUMBER      NOT NULL
    , primary key (proj_id, event_seq)
    , event_codeNUMBER       NOT NULL REFERENCES event_codes
    , event_date dateonly   NOT NULL
    );
```

Now, in order to insert an event into this table, we must use the following syntax:

```
INSERT INTO events VALUES ( 1, 1, 1, dateonly(trunc(sysdate));
```

The function dateonly in the above line is the *default constructor function* for the object type dateonly. This function is built for you when you create the type, and it cannot be overridden. This is another disappointment because, at first glance, the constructor function offers a natural mechanism for constraining the values being assigned. If we need to refer to the event_date in a select list or predicate clause, then we must refer to the type's member attribute by name. For example:

```
SELECT proj_id
     , event_code
  FROM events
 WHERE event_date.value >= '01-MAR-98';
```

Our types may also include member procedures and member functions. Oracle permits the creation of the special member functions, ORDER and MAP, so that the SQL engine can test whether one instance of a type is greater than or less than another instance of the same type. ORDER and MAP are described a bit later in this chapter, but first we need to point out that the ability to perform comparisons on ADTs does nothing to reduce the syntactic complexity of comparing an ADT with a literal. An alternative form of the previous example is:

```
SELECT proj_id
     , event_code
  FROM events
 WHERE event_date >= date_only('01-MAR-98');
```

WARNING Although Oracle provides the syntax CREATE OR REPLACE TYPE, there is an important restriction you need to be aware of before you get too far down the road designing and implementing tables that use ADTs. You can't make any changes at all to the definition of a TYPE which is currently in use (i.e., which is referenced in the definition of a table or of another type.) Eventually, schema maintenance products (such as BMC's PATROL DB-Alter for Oracle) will build the job required to simulate changes to TYPE definitions, and these jobs will perform all the required unloading, dropping, recreating, and reloading just as they do at present for changes to conventional tables. For the time being, any DBA who is administering a database which uses ADTs is pretty much on his own if a type definition has to be changed.

Methods

So far our examples have shown only types which define storage. However, types may also contain executable code in the form of methods which may be member procedures or member functions. These operate within the context of a particular instance of a type, and they can use the data values assigned to the attributes of the type. You can use these methods for any type of processing that you want to associate with the type. The example below expands the type staff_assignment_o to have a member function which returns the cost of the assignment:

```
CREATE OR REPLACE TYPE staff_assignment_o AS OBJECT
    ( staff_id    NUMBER
    , start_on    DATE
    , end_on      DATE
    , recover_at NUMBER
    , MEMBER FUNCTION cost RETURN NUMBER
    );

CREATE OR REPLACE TYPE BODY staff_assignment_o IS
    MEMBER FUNCTION cost RETURN NUMBER IS
    BEGIN
-- ignore the problem of non-working days
```

```
    -- could add lookup to working days table
    -- and to staff absence table
        RETURN ((end_on - start_on) * recover_at);
      END;
END;
```

We have already seen that each type has its own constructor method; this method has the same name as the type name and its default cannot be overridden. Two further special methods are the MAP and ORDER methods, and each type may only have one of these defined. Oracle uses whichever of MAP and ORDER are present to determine whether one instance of a type is greater than or less than another instance of a type. Let us assume that we decide to order our staff assignments by start date within staff member.

MAP function

The MAP function returns a number which can be used to rank the instances of the object type. In the case of our staff assignments, we may decide that the application will never contain start dates outside the range between January 1, 1996 and January 1, 2010. This is a period of 14 years and less than 10,000 days. Therefore, if we took the staff_id, multiplied it by 10,000, and then added the number of days between January 1, 1996 and the start date, we would get a number which would collate correctly.

```
MAP MEMBER FUNCTION MP RETURN NUMBER IS
BEGIN
   RETURN (  (staff_id * 10000)
           + (start_on.value - to_date
              ('01-JAN-1996', 'dd-MON-yyyy '));
   END;
```

MAP functions can at times be somewhat arbitrary, as in this example, but they are often a more efficient approach than ORDER functions. For a sort operation the MAP function need only be called once for each instance of the type.

ORDER function

The ORDER function takes another instance of the type as an argument and compares it with the current instance. It returns a negative integer if the current instance is less than the argument, zero if they are equal, and a positive integer if the current instance is greater than the argument.

```
ORDER MEMBER FUNCTION ORDER (a staff_assignment_o)
   RETURN NUMBER IS
BEGIN
   IF    (staff_id < a.staff_id)
   THEN RETURN -1;
```

```
    ELSIF (staff_id > a.staff_id)
    THEN RETURN +1;
    ELSE
      BEGIN
        IF     (start_on.value < a.start_on.value)
          RETURN -1;
        ELSIF (start_on.value > a.start_on.value)
          RETURN +1;
        ELSE
          RETURN 0;
        END IF;
    END IF;
END;
```

ORDER functions can be a little tedious to code, and may be called many thousands of times if used to support an ORDER BY clause in a SQL query. This is because the sort will require one call for each row comparison made during the sort operation—a minimum of $\log_2 N$ calls, where N is the number of rows to be sorted.

Collections

A collection is a set of occurrences of an abstract data type. Oracle8 supports two new types of collections: varying arrays (usually called VARRAYs) and nested tables. The two types are fundamentally different. Each has marked advantages and disadvantages, as we describe in the following sections.

VARRAYs

VARRAYs are a new data type implemented in both SQL and PL/SQL to support repeating groups. In their PL/SQL incarnation, their individual entries can be accessed using the same subscript syntax used for index-by tables. Individual entries in a VARRAY cannot be directly referenced in SQL, but an entire VARRAY within a row can be inserted from and fetched into a PL/SQL VARRAY variable.

VARRAYs are *ordered*, in the sense that the order in which the values are stored into the VARRAY will always be preserved, and they have a declared maximum number of entries. They cannot be nested—that is, the elements of a VARRAY cannot themselves contain VARRAYs.

The following DDL will put an array of up to 100 assignments into a project table:

```
CREATE OR REPLACE TYPE staff_assignment_v
  AS VARRAY (100) OF   staff_assignment_o;
```

```
CREATE TABLE projects
    ( proj_id    NUMBER       PRIMARY KEY
    , proj_name VARCHAR2(30) NOT NULL
    , manager    NUMBER       NOT NULL
          REFERENCES project_members
    , assignments staff_assignment_v -- up to 100 assignments
    , roi BFILE   -- leave the spreadsheet on the file server
    );
```

The type staff_assignment_v has a constructor function which takes up to 100 arguments, each of which must either be of type staff_assignment or be a NULL. Using the constructor function, the column can be populated from a SQL INSERT or UPDATE statement.

TIP   The selection of the value for the maximum dimension of a VARRAY is more important than it appears at first glance because Oracle uses the maximum possible length of the VARRAY to determine whether the value should be stored in-line with the data row or out-of-line in a separate segment.

The following code fragments show the retrieval of a VARRAY from a table into a PL/SQL variable:

```
...
    p_assigns staff_assignment_v;
...
    SELECT assignments INTO p_assigns
      FROM projects
     WHERE proj_id = 42;
...
```

The individual assignments can now be retrieved from the PL/SQL variable. This ability to handle short repeating groups without having to use a detail table can result in significant performance gains.

Nested Tables

Nested tables are exactly what they sound like: tables which are referenced within the context of a parent row. At present, Oracle8 supports one level of nesting. A parent table may contain more than one nested table, but no nested table may itself contain a nested table. This restriction is severe. It means, for example, that nested tables cannot be used to model a Customer object which contains Orders where those Orders contain Lines. The data in a nested table is held out-of-line from the parent row and is, like any table, unordered.

Each nested table can have any number of rows, have triggers created against it, and have indexes declared on it. Although a little hacking may allow you to partially circumvent the restriction, a nested table has no existence outside the context of its parent row. In addition, any index built on a nested table has the *object ID (OID)* of the parent row appended to the key so that direct access to a row of a nested table is impossible.

The following DDL creates a nested table of our staff assignments:

```
CREATE OR REPLACE TYPE staff_assignment_t
    AS TABLE OF          staff_assignment_o;

CREATE TABLE projects
    ( proj_id      NUMBER       PRIMARY KEY
    , proj_name    VARCHAR2(30) NOT NULL
    , manager      NUMBER       NOT NULL
          REFERENCES project_members
    , assignments staff_assignment_t --any number of assignments
    , roi          BFILE   -- leave the spreadsheet on fileserver)
    NESTED TABLE assignments STORE AS project_assignments;
```

Note that the NESTED TABLE clause is mandatory—unusually for Oracle, no arbitrary name is invented by default.

By using nested tables rather than VARRAYs we can use SQL to reference all of our data, but the extensions to the SQL syntax may take a little time to get used to, and they are certainly not supported by many current tools. Here is an example:

```
INSERT INTO THE
    (SELECT assignments FROM projects WHERE proj_id = 555)
    VALUES (34, '01-SEP-96', '30-SEP-96', 2000);
```

As stated above, every operation on the nested table must be carried out within the context of a parent row; in this case, the new SQL keyword, THE, signals a query which identifies the parent.

Which Collection Type?

When should you use collections? And which type of collection (VARRAY or nested table) should you use?

If you need to be able to select a parent type on the basis of the properties of its children, then don't use collections at all. Indexed access on a foreign key is impossible with either type of collection. For example, if you want to be able to retrieve all of the projects to which a particular employee is assigned, collections are only appropriate if you are willing to scan all of the projects in turn. This is a major drawback for many applications.

Suppose that you can deal with this restriction and that your goal is to be able to handle a small repeating group of items whose structure is known to the SQL engine but whose individual values are opaque at the SQL level. In this case, use VARRAYs. One real-world example which comes to mind is the need to hold each of the 48 half-hourly readings from a power meter (an example from Chapter 2). These readings have no individual significance except that they must be retained for audit purposes and that they are passed to a function which computes the day's cost from the set of readings. This function could, of course, be a member function. The data can be stored in the database using the constructor function from within standard INSERT or UPDATE statements, but you will need PL/SQL or C/C++ code to query it. The data will be held with the rest of the row, with a fairly low storage overhead.

Suppose that you can accept the restriction on not selecting parents on the basis of the properties of their children and that your goal is to be able to handle a semi-infinite set of items whose structure is not only known to the SQL engine, but whose values can be discretely inspected and set through the SQL engine. In this case, consider nested tables. However, remember that the SQL syntax is deeply foreign to the current generation of programmers with relational database experience.

Using collections may yield some performance benefits for groups of tables which are subject to heavy insert operations where the master and detail(s) are populated at the same time. By grouping them in a collection, you can reduce housekeeping overhead, especially for VARRAYs that are relatively short and are therefore stored in-line. However, we have not done any extensive testing to prove this assertion.

The nested table rows will be held in a separate table from the parent row, and an index is required. The object ID (OID) of the parent row is stored with each child row, and the total storage overhead should be comparable to that of the equivalent traditional master/detail table structure.

Object Views

Object views allow standard relational tables, and optionally object tables, to be joined within a view. The view has the external appearance of being an object table and, as such, may contain either or both of the new collection types (VARRAYs and nested tables). In theory, object views could be extremely useful; they allow an object-oriented application to use a standard relational data server, removing the need for the OO code to perform object assembly from the relational tables and moving that function into the view mechanism.

Sadly for the readers of this book, we expect that the facility offered by object views is likely to be the exact opposite of what you need. If your background is in relational rather than object technology, we'd guess that you don't have any tools that are able to operate through Oracle's client-side cache. As a result, object views are unlikely to be of any great use to you. However, as such tools become available, we are confident that object views will become increasingly important.

NOTE   One interesting aspect of an object view is that it allows two tables with a master-detail relationship to be projected as a single table (based on the parent) to which has been added a VARRAY to represent the child. In this case, there are no storage management implications to handling a very long VARRAY. However, if you are the programmer or DBA who is constructing the view, remember that VARRAYs are ordered and nested tables are not.

Looking Ahead

Ask any object guru what the cornerstones of object orientation are, and he will be likely to cite the following:

Encapsulation

The ability to interact with an object (a table, a method, anything) without having to know anything more about it than is absolutely necessary. Thus when we code:

```
SELECT dept.deptno FROM emp;
```

we do not need to know whether emp is a table or a view, or whether dept.deptno is a column or a member function. We do not know whether emp is in the current schema or whether a synonym points us to another schema, another database, or even a foreign data server through Oracle's heterogeneous option (the Oracle8 name for the former transparent gateways).

Inheritance

This concept is bound up with the idea of subclasses or subtypes; the idea is that you should be able to describe a class or type such as vehicle and then describe a subtype such as motorbike which, by default, has all of the attributes and methods of vehicle but which may supply attributes and methods of its own. PL/SQL does not support subtypes.

(Dynamic) Polymorphism

Gives the ability to code methods which will act differently depending on the datatypes of their arguments. PL/SQL already has *overloading*, which is polymorphism applied at compile time. Dynamic polymorphism, which is missing from PL/SQL, is not possible in a strongly typed language without subtypes.

Message passing

Requests for any service should be made by passing a message to the service, addressing it by name. This has long been a feature of SQL*Net (now Net8).

When John Spiers was Marketing Manager of Oracle UK, he used to give a most amusing and convincing presentation in which he supported the assertion that his cat was object-oriented. Of course, at that time Oracle made no claims to having object support, and at least one of their competitors used this fact to try to differentiate their product from the Oracle server. Now, although Oracle8 claims to have object support, it scores only 50% when measured against the four cornerstones. Even without the object support, Oracle was pretty strong on encapsulation and message passing, and with object support, it simply makes no attempt to provide either inheritance or dynamic polymorphism. As we've seen earlier in this chapter, there are a series of disappointments in the support provided within the type system.

At this point in time, we can't recommend the use of Oracle8's current object support within any normal enterprise application. The support itself is incomplete; the syntax is complex; and very few of the commonly used toolsets can cope with it even in pass-through mode (let alone actively support it). We do expect that object views will be used in a limited number of projects which are already using OO techniques, and that this technology will be effective in delivering virtual objects of limited complexity into a client-side cache.

In writing this book, we spent (some would say wasted) some time discussing how much space we should give to explaining the features that Oracle8 *does not* have—since we expect that what you need is help in designing for what the new release *does* have. In the end, we decided that a long essay on the features that an ideal OO database might have was out of place in a book about a relational engine.

Oracle8 may not satisfy OO purists, but how much does this really matter? Oracle8 is still based on an underlying relational model. Clearly, any move toward an object model will be a slow metamorphosis that won't hinder users who are happy to stay relational. Oracle's move toward object orientation is more apparent in its Network Computer Architecture (NCA) which allows users to plug cartridges (which are very similar in concept to applets) into the database or into a client application.

We're not anti-object—honestly, we're not. Nor are we anti-Oracle. It is just that the object support which we have seen and have been able to try in Oracle8 right now simply does not stack up. We're not completely unhappy with Oracle8. The toolset issue is secondary and, as we said earlier in this chapter, we see no reason why an object-oriented application can't use a structured, decomposed store as its data repository. Once we get a persistent store with the following features:

- Subclasses
- Inheritance
- Dynamic polymorphism
- The ability to place declarative constraints on attributes of object types
- The ability to specify constructor functions
- Default invocation of constructor functions (maybe)

then we'll expect to be very interested in leveraging these features in our own designs.

For the moment, we do not expect to be using Oracle8 object support in our own projects. Nevertheless, we do expect that we will find a number of uses for LOBs to hold data whose structure does not need to be defined in the Oracle data dictionary. In some cases, we also expect to be coding significant PL/SQL functions, along the lines of the DBMS_LOB package (described in Chapter 4), to allow procedural access to the structures inside the LOBs.

6

Tool Support for Oracle8

At the time this book is going to press, the marketing message from Oracle Corporation about tool support for Oracle8 is still rather confusing. What is clear is that there is currently no support for relational tools to support object data. Unfortunately, the Oracle toolset of Developer/2000 Release 1.3/1.4 and Oracle Power Objects won't be able to take advantage of most of the new features of Oracle8. Systems built on relational tools will benefit from increased scalability and performance, but little else. There will be support for many of the features in Programmer/2000 (the Oracle pre-compilers and the Oracle Call Interface or OCI). What Oracle is providing in Oracle8 is basically a means of making relational data accessible to object-oriented tools through the provision of object views. This means that object-oriented development tools such as Rational Rose will be able to view legacy relational data in object form.

This chapter takes a quick look at Oracle's current support for various tools and technology from the perspective of Oracle8.

Sedona

Most people in the Oracle community expected that Oracle would announce its new generation tools (code-named Sedona) at the same time as the Oracle8 announcement. Sedona was to be an object-oriented development suite that would exploit the object features of Oracle8 and would also allow the specification and deployment of distributed objects using standards such as CORBA and COM/DCOM. Sedona has now been delayed for at least a year, and recent statements from Oracle have suggested that it may never become a product.

Why has this happened? It appears that the developers of Oracle's own application suite of Financial and Human Resources packages have not been impressed with the Sedona product. Another factor was the lack of Java support; project Sedona was started before Java and NCA were conceived, and to some extent, it has been overtaken by technology. A major reevaluation of Sedona is now underway and if the product does re-emerge, it will probably be built more around the Jbuilder Java-based technology that Oracle has licensed from Borland.

In the meantime, where does that leave us when we have to select a toolset for an Oracle8 development? Traditionally the tools have always lagged slightly behind in supporting the functionality of the database. For this reason, the adoption of the new technology is rather slow since developers tend to wait for the tools to catch up. Only those who develop applications using 3GL languages (such as C and C++) will be able to take advantage of the new features in the immediate to near future.

Developer/2000

The current versions of Developer/2000 are built around Oracle7 relational technology. You will be able to use Developer/2000 to develop applications to run against an Oracle8 database, but you won't be able to use a lot of the new features. In particular:

- Developer/2000 Release 1.3 still has a PL/SQL engine stuck at Version 1. This means that you cannot define record types or PL/SQL tables, let alone any of the new type support in PL/SQL8 (the version that comes with Oracle8).

- Developer/2000 Release 2.0 will probably have a PL/SQL engine based on PL/SQL 2.x which is a step in the right direction but is still lacking support for any of the new features of Oracle8. Furthermore, Forms 5.0 (a component of Developer/2000 Release 2.0) allows us to base a block on a PL/SQL package rather than on a relational object such as a table or a view. This may enable us to exploit some of the features of Oracle8, but will still require data to be returned to the client in tabular form.

- Designer/2000 does not currently utilize the advanced features of Net8 such as connection pooling and multiplexed connections.

- Currently, there is no support for object types, object views, LOBS, BFILEs, nested tables, or variable arrays. These are planned for a future version, but no dates have been announced.

- One of the main complaints we hear from users of Developer/2000 is that the runtime has a very large footprint (in other words, it requires a lot of client memory). This does not seem to make it an appropriate tool for deploying on a Network Computer (NC).

- We know of no plan for Developer/2000 to utilize client-side cache.

Forms and Reports can call out to *user exits* which can be developed using C or C++. User exit code can directly write to any items on the form and can pop up its own windows. So you could develop code around strictly relational objects using forms and call out to user exits to handle any nonrelational aspects. For instance, suppose that you had a table containing a VARRAY. You can base a block in the form on a view that excludes the VARRAY and manage the content of the VARRAY with a C or C++ user exit that uses the appropriate OCI calls. A messy solution, but it may be one of the few options in the short term. Since Oracle Forms began supporting PL/SQL the user exit facility has had a bit of a demise, but it may be about to make a strong comeback.

One facility in Oracle8 that new applications written in Designer/2000 could exploit is server-based queuing using the Advanced Queuing Support (Oracle/AQ). Transactional triggers (on-insert, on-update, on-lock, and on-delete) can be written to replace the default behavior of a form with a call to the DBMS_AQ package, to enqueue a message. This could improve response time in a heavy transaction processing system and is a viable alternative to teleprocessing monitors such as CICS and Tuxedo.

Designer/2000

Like Developer/2000, Designer/2000 has always lagged behind the Oracle kernel. There was a long delay between the launch of Oracle7 and support for Version 7 DDL syntax from the Designer/2000 generator. Many a shell script was written to hack the Version 6 CREATE TABLE statements that were generated into the Version 7 equivalent. We hope the wait won't be as long this time.

Designer/2000 Version 2.0 will support the new objects inherent in Oracle8 and allow them to be specified in the repository. It is currently planned that release 2.0 of this product will allow the specification in the database design of:

- Deferred constraint checking
- LOBs

- Index-only tables

- Referenced and embedded objects

- User-defined data types

Defining these in a repository seems like the way to go. In the meantime, the same reservations that we expressed about Developer/2000 apply, in the short term, to any code generated by Designer/2000. The code will only support Oracle7 features, although you can run the designer on an Oracle8 database.

Most people anticipate that the diagramming and notational convention for defining objects will be an extension of the *Unified Modeling Language (UML)* which is an emerging standard for object modeling currently being defined by the Object Management Group (OMG).

We expect that in Designer/2000 Release 2.0, the database design wizard will be extended to allow more implementation choice. In certain cases, it will give the option of using either a relational or an object structure. For instance, a parent-child construct in a logical model could be implemented in a variety of ways:

- Conventionally, using foreign keys

- Conventionally, using foreign keys with the addition of object views

- As a VARRAY of REFs in the parent (with each entry pointing to a child)

- As a nested table

The code generation of Designer/2000 will also need to be brought up to date to support Oracle8 features in generated code on both the client and server sides. The client code generation is, of course, dependent on the new features in Developer/2000 and may be some time coming. There will definitely be support for generating C++ class definitions for all the objects in the repository.

Object Designer

To plug some of the gaps in Designer/2000, a new design tool called Object Designer is expected to be released shortly. It is based on the existing Database Designer tool, but also has extensions specifically aimed at Oracle8 and object support. Object Designer will let you model, design, and generate objects from a GUI front end. It will enable designers to specify embedded and referenced object types including nested tables and variable arrays. We expect that the Object Designer will allow for the specification and integration of NCA data cartridges.

Object Designer will also be capable of generating C++ class definitions for objects which provide transparent persistency for objects, thus shielding the programmer from the complexity of the underlying database. There will be a class definition generated for each abstract data type along with a mapping that allows the types to be referenced as persistent data stores.

Object Designer will also use UML conventions to represent objects.

An important feature of the Object Designer will be its ability to reverse-engineer definitions from an existing database schema (including Oracle7 schemas) and to create a type model from it. This type model can then be used to generate an object schema.

SQL*Plus

SQL*Plus is not a tool for application development, but in all releases of Oracle from Version 4 (where it was called UFI) to Oracle7, it was an ideal tool for trying out the syntax, for ad hoc database inquiry and maintenance, for DBAs to produce their columnar reports of object space usage, and for very little else.

In Oracle8, many features of the object support cannot be directly exercised from SQL*Plus because they cannot be directly exercised from SQL itself. The handling of VARRAYs is a good example. If SQL*Plus is viewed as a tool for running PL/SQL as well as SQL, then a number of the object features become available through PL/SQL packages. PL/SQL also has a mechanism for handling VARRAYs. We doubt, however, that very many people are going to be happy with the amount of work which is required to operate in this manner.

PL/SQL

For many years now, PL/SQL has been the flagship procedural language for Oracle. Developers are familiar with it, and it has been extended with the addition of libraries to support Oracle WebServer, file I/O, and calls to external APIs—among many other things. With the latest release (PL/SQL8), Oracle has further strengthened PL/SQL. This release supports most of the features of Oracle8, with the exception of client-side cache (see Chapter 5, *Objects*, for more details).

PL/SQL is the only language that can be stored and executed within the database itself. However, as with SQL*Plus, we can't conceive of writing an entire application in PL/SQL. It is a very good tool for server-side development, but it has no facilities for managing the user interface.

Oracle has recently announced that it intends to support native Java in the database from Release 8.1 onwards. So at that point, Java will become a viable alternative to the proprietary PL/SQL as the server language. This will be an attractive proposition to development shops that want to standardize on a single language that is an industry-wide standard. But until Release 8.1 (whenever that is), there is no choice. We anticipate that a number of third parties will seize the opportunity and offer PL/SQL-to-Java conversion tools. So if you prefer Java but need to develop on Release 8.0, don't fret too much.

C, C++, and OCI

To fully leverage the functionality of Oracle8, you will have to develop your application suite in C or C++. This is not an attractive option for most projects. Don't get us wrong: we love C and C++, but realistically they can't be developed as rapidly as a 4GL and are generally harder to maintain. Even if you employ a rich set of classes for screen and widget handling and you use drag-and-drop wizards to help you design screens, there is still a lot of code to write to get a fully functioning screen (compared with Oracle Forms or Visual Basic anyway).

To some extent, use of the class generator from Object Designer may alleviate some of the programming burden by making database access transparent. The developer simply has to manipulate and call methods of persistent objects. Everything else (including the management of the client-side cache) is handled by generated code.

Approaches to Extracting the Data

A C or C++ program that needs to interface with Oracle data can do so in one of three ways:

1. Use the pre-compiler to convert embedded SQL statements into server API calls.

2. Make explicit calls to an ODBC driver.

3. Make explicit calls to the Oracle Call Interface (OCI).

To gain full access to the Oracle8 server object capabilities, the code must use OCI. OCI is a low-level interface to Oracle that many predicted would be discontinued since using the precompiler is quicker and easier. However, OCI has always given the programmer more control over the database interface and has proved many people wrong. Now, far from being obsolete, it is currently at the forefront of Oracle development tools.

OCI is a bit daunting for those who have never used it, and you would probably want to think twice about imposing it on a team of inexperienced developers just so you can exploit the Oracle8 facilities that aren't supported by any other tool!

Reasons to Use OCI

Despite its complexity, OCI offers a number of significant technical advantages for software projects. We expect that the software tools industry will use it rather than ODBC for Oracle-specific layers. People from within Oracle have told us that a policy decision has been made that Oracle Corporation itself will switch to using OCI as the interface between the company's own C and C++-based products which call the database server. In the past, these products have been coded to use a lower-level interface generally referred to as UPI (user program interface). As no documentation on this interface has ever been officially released to users, you might consider this name to be something of a contradiction.

Oracle's decision is important, however, because up to now UPI has been the only mechanism which gave access to all of the features of the Oracle server. Over the years, a number of the features available at the UPI level (such as savepoints) have been externalized in the SQL syntax. Oracle is now saying that all UPI features will be available at the OCI level. If this is true, then the repertoire should include BECOME USER, a UPI call which is used by IMPort to set up data dictionary entries correctly.

Java

The Java bandwagon continues to roll. All major suppliers are Java-enabling their tools, and Oracle Corporation is no different. Witness the company's recent licensing of the Borland JBuilder tool. You can currently use Java to access the Oracle8 database through one of the many available JDBC drivers. Like their ODBC counterparts, most JDBC drivers support ANSI 92 SQL and thus won't have intrinsic support for any of the object or extended features of Oracle8. It is likely that all levels of NCA will fully support Java applets and Oracle will soon allow you to execute the emerging J/SQL against an Oracle8 database. (J/SQL is a product under development by Oracle which will let you embed SQL in Java; this will give you functionality similar to that available via precompiler programming today.)

If you have to choose one language or technology to "hang your hat on" and invest time getting proficient at, then we recommend Java. We are fairly confident that Java will be the database access technology of tomorrow. And remember, Oracle has said that Java will soon be offered as an alternative to PL/SQL for writing code that resides and executes within the database engine. (Great word, *soon..* You should have plenty of time to learn Java even if you can only spare a couple of hours a month.)

Other Tools

Most third-party tools (e.g., Visual Basic, PowerBuilder, Delphi, etc.) rely on ODBC to access the Oracle database. Some can utilize Oracle Objects for OLE (OO4O), which is a bit like ODBC with Oracle extensions (or lock-ins to an Oracle back end). ODBC supports pure ANSI SQL and, as such, will object to any Oracle extensions. This made it difficult to write efficient and feature-rich applications with Oracle7 because any Oracle extensions to SQL (such as DECODE and most SQL functions) are not supported and are rejected as invalid syntax.

Luckily, there is a workaround to this restriction—by using a mode called "pass-through," the ODBC driver allows SQL to pass to the server without attempting to do validation. Even with this mode, there are restrictions— simple things like returning values to the client from a stored function or procedure just wasn't possible with ODBC (although it will be with OO4O).

These tools may describe themselves as object-oriented development environments, and we won't argue about the merits of such a description. But note that they still rely on SQL alone to communicate with the database and have no support for a persistent data store which handles complex objects.

Conclusion

We believe that the scarcity of tools that support the Oracle8 object features will lead to a slow early uptake of these features. Most development projects simply can't afford the extra time involved in developing the entire suite in C/C++ with low-level OCI calls. Most of the early takers of Oracle8 will deploy it purely as a faster and more scaleable relational database. The partitioning support which we describe in Chapter 4 can be exploited without application changes and will be a sufficient incentive for many sites to undertake the migration. As the product matures and the tools catch up with their support, then we expect there to be a flood of users. Based on our previous experience, we expect that this catch-up phase could easily take the rest of the century—so it is just as well that Oracle7 dates support the year 2000.

About the Authors

Dave Ensor is manager of Worldwide Solutions, PATROL R&D with BMC Software, where his roles are assisting customers in their use of both BMC's PATROL product and the Oracle Server and feeding the results of his field work back into product planning. He has more than 30 years of IT experience and has been involved with the design and performance issues surrounding Oracle since 1987. For many years he led Oracle Worldwide's Performance Studies Group based in the U.K., which provided consultancy support to both customer and internal projects with critical performance requirements. Dave is well known as a speaker on performance management and design; he presents his papers at user conferences and writes and delivers one-day seminars. He lives in the U.K. just outside London, but spends much of the year travelling to user sites and meetings. In his spare time he also travels, but in this case without his laptop and with his wife. He can be reached at *dave_ensor@compuserve.com.*

Ian Stevenson is a freelance consultant specializing in database design and development. He has worked with database technology for 19 years, starting with early hierarchical models. He worked for Oracle (U.K.) for two years in Post-Sales Support and Human Resources Development. This is where he formed his friendship with Dave Ensor. Ian has a first class honours degree in Mathematics from the University of Southampton and is a member of the British Computer Society. He is married to Brenda and has two children, Todd and Tara. He is a fanatic supporter of the Southampton football club. He can be contacted at *ian@westmail.demon.co.uk.*

Dave and Ian are coauthors of *Oracle Design* (O'Reilly & Associates, 1996).

Colophon

The insect featured on the cover of *Oracle Design* is a dragonfly of the family Libellulidae, or common skimmer. Dragonflies, along with damselflies, comprise the order Odonata. Dragonflies are predatory insects. Young dragonflies are aquatic insects. They are equipped with a unique "jet propulsion" ability. By drawing water in through their gills, located in the posterior of their abdomens, and quickly forcing it out again they are able to powerfully propel themselves across the water surface. This technique is used in emergencies when a quick getaway is called for.

Mature dragonflies are among nature's most impressive fliers. Because they achieve great speed and power relative to their size, their flying techniques have been studied extensively by aviation engineers. Dragonflies are able to fly as fast as 35 miles per hour, and to perform impressive mid-air acrobatics. Unlike most flying insects, dragonflies operate their front and rear wings independently. They twist their wings slightly on the downstroke, thus creating mini-whirlwinds that move over the wing surface faster than still air would.

Adult dragonflies catch and eat their prey while flying. They fly with their long, bristle-covered legs bent in front of them, forming something like a basket, which they use to scoop up other insects. Dragonflies are quite popular with humans both because of their beauty and grace and because their diet is largely made up of mosquitoes and flies.

Edie Freedman designed the cover of this book, using a 19th-century engraving from the Dover Pictorial Archive. The cover layout was produced with Quark XPress 3.3 using the ITC Garamond font. Whenever possible, our books use RepKover[TM], a durable and flexible lay-flat binding. If the page count exceeds RepKover's limit, perfect binding is used.

The inside layout was designed by Edie Freedman and Nancy Priest and implemented in FrameMaker by Mike Sierra. The text and heading fonts are ITC Garamond Light and Garamond Book. The illustrations that appear in the book were created in Macromedia Freehand by Chris Reilley and Robert Romano. This colophon was written by Clairemarie Fisher O'Leary.

More Titles from O'Reilly

Database

Oracle PL/SQL Programming, 2nd Edition

By Steven Feuerstein with Bill Pribyl
2nd Edition October 1997 (est.)
1056 pages (est.), plus disk
ISBN 1-56592-335-9

The first edition of *Oracle PL/SQL
Programming* has become the
bible for PL/SQL developers. This
new edition updates the Oracle8
material and includes chapters on
Oracle8 object types, object views, collections, external
procedures, and large object types and functions. It also
covers new strategies for tuning, tracing, and debugging
PL/SQL programs, and offers many new programs on the
accompanying disk.

Oracle8 Design Tips

By Dave Ensor & Ian Stevenson
1st Edition September 1997
130 pages, ISBN 1-56592-361-8

The newest version of the Oracle
DBMS, Oracle8, offers some dramatically different features from previous
versions, including better scalability,
reliability, and security; an object-
relational model; additional data-
types; and more. To get peak performance out of an
Oracle8 system, databases and code need to be designed
with these new features in mind. This small book tells
Oracle designers and developers just what they need to
know to use the Oracle8 features to best advantage.

Mastering Oracle Power Objects

By Rick Greenwald & Robert Hoskin
1st Edition March 1997, 508 pages,
plus disk, ISBN 1-56592-239-5

The first book to cover Power
Objects Version 2, a cross-platform
development tool that greatly sim-
plifies the development of client/
server database applications.
Aimed at developers, it provides in-
depth coverage of advanced features, including lists,
reports, built-in methods, object-oriented principles,
global functions and messaging, and use of PL/SQL and
the World Wide Web. The accompanying disk contains
practical and complete examples that will help you build
working applications, right now.

Oracle Performance Tuning, 2nd Edition

By Mark Gurry & Peter Corrigan
2nd Edition November 1996, 964 pages,
plus disk, ISBN 1-56592-237-9

Performance tuning is crucial in
any modern relational database
management system. The first edition of this book has become a
classic for developers, DBAs, and
everyone who cares about improv-
ing the performance of an Oracle system. This edition is a
complete revision, with 400 pages of new material on new
Oracle features, including parallel server, parallel query,
Oracle Performance Pack, disk striping and mirroring,
RAID, MPPs, SMPs, distributed databases, backup and
recovery, and much more. Includes disk.

Oracle Design

By Dave Ensor & Ian Stevenson
1st Edition March 1997
546 pages, 1-56592-268-9

This book looks thoroughly at the
field of Oracle relational database
design, an often-neglected area of
Oracle, but one that has an enormous impact on the ultimate
power and performance of a
system. Focuses on both database and code design,
including such special design areas as data models,
denormalization, the use of keys and indexes, temporal
data, special architectures (client/server, distributed database, parallel processing), and data warehouses.

Advanced Oracle PL/SQL Programming with Packages

By Steven Feuerstein,
1st Edition Oct.1996, 690 pages,
plus diskette, ISBN 1-56592-238-7

This book explains the best way to
construct packages, a powerful
part of Oracle's PL/SQL procedural
language that can dramatically
improve your programming pro-
ductivity and code quality, while
preparing you for object-oriented development in Oracle
technology. It comes with PL/Vision software, a library of
PL/SQL packages developed by the author, and takes you
behind the scenes as it examines how and why the
PL/Vision packages were implemented the way they were.

O'REILLY™

How to stay in touch with O'Reilly

1. Visit Our Award-Winning Site

http://www.oreilly.com/

★"Top 100 Sites on the Web" —*PC Magazine*
★"Top 5% Web sites" —*Point Communications*
★"3-Star site" —*The McKinley Group*

Our web site contains a library of comprehensive product information (including book excerpts and tables of contents), downloadable software, background articles, interviews with technology leaders, links to relevant sites, book cover art, and more. File us in your Bookmarks or Hotlist!

2. Join Our Email Mailing Lists

New Product Releases

To receive automatic email with brief descriptions of all new O'Reilly products as they are released, send email to:
listproc@online.oreilly.com
Put the following information in the first line of your message (*not* in the Subject field):
subscribe oreilly-news "Your Name" of "Your Organization" (for example: subscribe oreilly-news Kris Webber of Fine Enterprises)

O'Reilly Events

If you'd also like us to send information about trade show events, special promotions, and other O'Reilly events, send email to:
listproc@online.oreilly.com
Put the following information in the first line of your message (*not* in the Subject field):
subscribe oreilly-events "Your Name" of "Your Organization"

3. Get Examples from Our Books via FTP

There are two ways to access an archive of example files from our books:

Regular FTP

* ftp to:
  ftp.oreilly.com
  (login: anonymous
  password: your email address)
* Point your web browser to:
  ftp://ftp.oreilly.com/

FTPMAIL

* Send an email message to:
  ftpmail@online.oreilly.com
  (Write "help" in the message body)

4. Visit Our Gopher Site

* Connect your gopher to:
  gopher.oreilly.com

* Point your web browser to:
  gopher://gopher.oreilly.com/

* Telnet to:
  **gopher.oreilly.com
  login: gopher**

5. Contact Us via Email

order@oreilly.com
To place a book or software order online. Good for North American and international customers.

subscriptions@oreilly.com
To place an order for any of our newsletters or periodicals.

books@oreilly.com
General questions about any of our books.

software@oreilly.com
For general questions and product information about our software. Check out O'Reilly Software Online at **http://software.oreilly.com/** for software and technical support information. Registered O'Reilly software users send your questions to:
website-support@oreilly.com

cs@oreilly.com
For answers to problems regarding your order or our products.

booktech@oreilly.com
For book content technical questions or corrections.

proposals@oreilly.com
To submit new book or software proposals to our editors and product managers.

international@oreilly.com
For information about our international distributors or translation queries. For a list of our distributors outside of North America check out:
http://www.oreilly.com/www/order/country.html

O'Reilly & Associates, Inc.
101 Morris Street, Sebastopol, CA 95472 USA
TEL   707-829-0515 or 800-998-9938
          (6am to 5pm PST)
FAX   707-829-0104

O'REILLY™

Titles from O'Reilly

Please note that upcoming titles are displayed in italic.

WEB PROGRAMMING

Apache: The Definitive Guide
Building Your Own Web
  Conferences
Building Your Own Website
Building Your Own Win-CGI
  Programs
CGI Programming for the World
  Wide Web
Designing for the Web
HTML: The Definitive Guide
JavaScript: The Definitive Guide,
  2nd Ed.
Learning Perl
Programming Perl, 2nd Ed.
Mastering Regular Expressions
WebMaster in a Nutshell
Web Security & Commerce
*Web Client Programming with
  Perl*
World Wide Web Journal

USING THE INTERNET

Smileys
The Future Does Not Compute
The Whole Internet User's Guide
  & Catalog
The Whole Internet for Win 95
Using Email Effectively
Bandits on the Information
  Superhighway

JAVA SERIES

Exploring Java
Java AWT Reference
Java Fundamental Classes
  Reference
Java in a Nutshell
Java Language Reference
Java Network Programming
Java Threads
Java Virtual Machine

SOFTWARE

WebSite™ 1.1
WebSite Professional™
Building Your Own Web
  Conferences
WebBoard™
PolyForm™
Statisphere™

SONGLINE GUIDES

NetActivism   NetResearch
Net Law   NetSuccess
NetLearning   NetTravel
Net Lessons

SYSTEM ADMINISTRATION

Building Internet Firewalls
Computer Crime: A Crimefighter's
  Handbook
Computer Security Basics
DNS and BIND, 2nd Ed.
Essential System Administration,
  2nd Ed.
Getting Connected: The Internet
  at 56K and Up
*Internet Server Administration
  with Windows NT*
Linux Network Administrator's
  Guide
Managing Internet Information
  Services
Managing NFS and NIS
Networking Personal Computers
  with TCP/IP
Practical UNIX & Internet
  Security, 2nd Ed.
PGP: Pretty Good Privacy
sendmail, 2nd Ed.
sendmail Desktop Reference
System Performance Tuning
TCP/IP Network Administration
termcap & terminfo
Using & Managing UUCP
Volume 8: X Window System
  Administrator's Guide
Web Security & Commerce

UNIX

Exploring Expect
Learning VBScript
Learning GNU Emacs, 2nd Ed.
Learning the bash Shell
Learning the Korn Shell
Learning the UNIX Operating
  System
Learning the vi Editor
Linux in a Nutshell
Making TeX Work
Linux Multimedia Guide
Running Linux, 2nd Ed.
SCO UNIX in a Nutshell
sed & awk, 2nd Edition
Tcl/Tk Tools
UNIX in a Nutshell: System V
  Edition
UNIX Power Tools
Using csh & tsch
When You Can't Find Your UNIX
  System Administrator
Writing GNU Emacs Extensions

WEB REVIEW STUDIO SERIES

Gif Animation Studio
Shockwave Studio

WINDOWS

Dictionary of PC Hardware and
  Data Communications Terms
Inside the Windows 95 Registry
Inside the Windows 95 File
  System
Windows Annoyances
*Windows NT File System
  Internals*
Windows NT in a Nutshell

PROGRAMMING

Advanced Oracle PL/SQL
  Programming
Applying RCS and SCCS
C++: The Core Language
Checking C Programs with lint
DCE Security Programming
Distributing Applications Across
  DCE & Windows NT
Encyclopedia of Graphics File
  Formats, 2nd Ed.
Guide to Writing DCE
  Applications
lex & yacc
Managing Projects with make
Mastering Oracle Power Objects
Oracle Design: The Definitive
  Guide
Oracle Performance Tuning, 2nd
  Ed.
Oracle PL/SQL Programming
Porting UNIX Software
POSIX Programmer's Guide
POSIX.4: Programming for the
  Real World
Power Programming with RPC
Practical C Programming
Practical C++ Programming
Programming Python
Programming with curses
Programming with GNU Software
Pthreads Programming
Software Portability with imake,
  2nd Ed.
Understanding DCE
Understanding Japanese
  Information Processing
UNIX Systems Programming for
  SVR4

BERKELEY 4.4 SOFTWARE DISTRIBUTION

4.4BSD System Manager's Manual
4.4BSD User's Reference Manual
4.4BSD User's Supplementary
  Documents
4.4BSD Programmer's Reference
  Manual
4.4BSD Programmer's
  Supplementary Documents
X Programming
Vol. 0: X Protocol Reference
  Manual
Vol. 1: Xlib Programming Manual
Vol. 2: Xlib Reference Manual
Vol. 3M: X Window System User's
  Guide, Motif Edition
Vol. 4M: X Toolkit Intrinsics
  Programming Manual, Motif
  Edition
Vol. 5: X Toolkit Intrinsics
  Reference Manual
Vol. 6A: Motif Programming
  Manual
Vol. 6B: Motif Reference Manual
Vol. 6C: Motif Tools
Vol. 8 : X Window System
  Administrator's Guide
Programmer's Supplement for
  Release 6
X User Tools
The X Window System in a
  Nutshell

CAREER & BUSINESS

Building a Successful Software
  Business
The Computer User's Survival
  Guide
Love Your Job!
Electronic Publishing on CD-ROM

TRAVEL

Travelers' Tales: Brazil
Travelers' Tales: Food
Travelers' Tales: France
Travelers' Tales: Gutsy Women
Travelers' Tales: India
Travelers' Tales: Mexico
Travelers' Tales: Paris
Travelers' Tales: San Francisco
Travelers' Tales: Spain
Travelers' Tales: Thailand
Travelers' Tales: A Woman's
  World

O'REILLY™

TO ORDER: **800-998-9938** • **order@oreilly.com** • **http://www.oreilly.com/**
OUR PRODUCTS ARE AVAILABLE AT A BOOKSTORE OR SOFTWARE STORE NEAR YOU.
FOR INFORMATION: **800-998-9938** • **707-829-0515** • **info@oreilly.com**

International Distributors

UK, Europe, Middle East and Northern Africa (except France, Germany, Switzerland, & Austria)

INQUIRIES
International Thomson Publishing Europe
Berkshire House
168-173 High Holborn
London WC1V 7AA, UK
Tel: 44-171-497-1422
Fax: 44-171-497-1426
Email: itpint@itps.co.uk

ORDERS
International Thomson Publishing Services, Ltd.
Cheriton House, North Way
Andover, Hampshire SP10 5BE, United Kingdom
Tel: 44-264-342-832 (UK)
Tel: 44-264-342-806
  (outside UK)
Fax: 44-264-364418 (UK)
Fax: 44-264-342761 (outside UK)
UK & Eire orders:
itpuk@itps.co.uk
International orders:
itpint@itps.co.uk

France

Editions Eyrolles
61 bd Saint-Germain
75240 Paris Cedex 05
France
Fax: 33-01-44-41-11-44

FRENCH LANGUAGE BOOKS
All countries except Canada
Tel: 33-01-44-41-46-16
Email: geodif@eyrolles.com

ENGLISH LANGUAGE BOOKS
Tel: 33-01-44-41-11-87
Email: distribution@eyrolles.com

Australia

WoodsLane Pty. Ltd.
7/5 Vuko Place, Warriewood NSW 2102
P.O. Box 935,
Mona Vale NSW 2103
Australia
Tel: 61-2-9970-5111
Fax: 61-2-9970-5002
Email: info@woodslane.com.au

Germany, Switzerland, and Austria

INQUIRIES
O'Reilly Verlag
Balthasarstr. 81
D-50670 Köln
Germany
Tel: 49-221-97-31-60-0
Fax: 49-221-97-31-60-8
Email: anfragen@oreilly.de

ORDERS
International Thomson Publishing
Königswinterer Straße 418
53227 Bonn, Germany
Tel: 49-228-97024 0
Fax: 49-228-441342
Email: order@oreilly.de

Asia (except Japan & India)

INQUIRIES
International Thomson Publishing Asia
60 Albert Street #15-01
Albert Complex
Singapore 189969
Tel: 65-336-6411
Fax: 65-336-7411

ORDERS
Telephone: 65-336-6411
Fax: 65-334-1617
thomson@signet.com.sg

New Zealand

WoodsLane New Zealand Ltd.
21 Cooks Street (P.O. Box 575)
Wanganui, New Zealand
Tel: 64-6-347-6543
Fax: 64-6-345-4840
Email: info@woodslane.com.au

Japan

O'Reilly Japan, Inc.
Kiyoshige Building 2F
12-Banchi, Sanei-cho
Shinjuku-ku
Tokyo 160 Japan
Tel: 81-3-3356-5227
Fax: 81-3-3356-5261
Email: kenji@oreilly.com

India

Computer Bookshop (India) PVT. LTD.
190 Dr. D.N. Road, Fort
Bombay 400 001 India
Tel: 91-22-207-0989
Fax: 91-22-262-3551
Email:
cbsbom@giasbm01.vsnl.net.in

The Americas

O'Reilly & Associates, Inc.
101 Morris Street
Sebastopol, CA 95472 U.S.A.
Tel: 707-829-0515
Tel: 800-998-9938 (U.S. & Canada)
Fax: 707-829-0104
Email: order@oreilly.com

Southern Africa

International Thomson Publishing Southern Africa
Building 18, Constantia Park
138 Sixteenth Road
P.O. Box 2459
Halfway House, 1685 South Africa
Tel: 27-11-805-4819
Fax: 27-11-805-3648

O'REILLY™

O'Reilly & Associates, Inc.
101 Morris Street
Sebastopol, CA 95472-9902
1-800-998-9938

Visit us online at:
http://www.ora.com/
orders@ora.com

O'REILLY WOULD LIKE TO HEAR FROM YOU

Which book did this card come from?

_____

Where did you buy this book?
- ❏ Bookstore   ❏ Computer Store
- ❏ Direct from O'Reilly   ❏ Class/seminar
- ❏ Bundled with hardware/software

❏ Other _____

What operating system do you use?
- ❏ UNIX   ❏ Macintosh
- ❏ Windows NT   ❏ PC(Windows/DOS)

❏ Other _____

What is your job description?
- ❏ System Administrator   ❏ Programmer
- ❏ Network Administrator   ❏ Educator/Teacher
- ❏ Web Developer

❏ Other _____

❏ Please send me O'Reilly's catalog, containing a complete listing of O'Reilly books and software.

Name _____ Company/Organization _____

Address _____

City _____ State _____ Zip/Postal Code _____ Country _____

Telephone _____ Internet or other email address (specify network) _____

Nineteenth century wood engraving
of a bear from the O'Reilly &
Associates Nutshell Handbook®
Using & Managing UUCP.

BUSINESS REPLY MAIL
FIRST CLASS MAIL   PERMIT NO. 80   SEBASTOPOL, CA

Postage will be paid by addressee

O'Reilly & Associates, Inc.
101 Morris Street
Sebastopol, CA 95472-9902